THE TR

THE WHOLE TRUTH AND NOTHING BUT THE TRUTH

WRITTEN BY IRENE DUNROE

love Irene Dunroe
(never eat a raw onion,
its bound to end in tears)
one of Charlies sayings
x x

Mojo Risin'
Publishing Ltd

Published in 2022 by Mojo Risin' Publishing Ltd
www.mojorisinpublishing.com

British Library Cataloguing in Publication Data:
A catalogue record for this book is available from
the British Library

ISBN-13:
978-1-9163867-9-2

Cover design
David Stanyer

Layout
Neil Jackson, Media Arts
www.media-arts.co.uk

Printed & bound by PrintGuy
Proudly published Up North

I dedicate this book to our son Michael, who has lived with this nightmare second by second with us.

To the memory of my lovely mum and Michael's nan, who walked alongside us both in support.

To the memory of Mrs Jones, who especially in those early years, was always ready to wipe away my tears.

God Bless you all.

Contents

Foreword By Charlie Salvador

I write this when I've not even read the manuscript as I know how my ex-wife rolls - with dignity and self respect. It's why I married her all these decades ago so I know in my heart this will be a great read. A true account of a real survivor.

This book will no doubt inspire thousands of women who end up fighting alone to survive. There's so many books on prisoners, but so few of the wives and partners left behind in a very dark place.

Irene and me have not met for well over 40 years. Obviously we are in touch by letter and phone. I'm still very fond of her and feel close. But our worlds are a million miles apart.

I wish her all the luck in the world and hope this book will show you all why I married this amazing woman. Let's face it, what armed robber would wear a pair of his wife's panties on a blag? Only one who idolised her (me). Those panties were supposed to have brought me luck. I think I picked the wrong colour!

Thanks Irene for making me smile and thanks for baring our son Michael.

Love and madness

Chapter One: Early Life – Before Charlie

"She came into this world as Irene Kelsey". How surreal was this! I was attending the funeral of the aunt I was named after and it felt as if I was at my own funeral. I thought what a good way to begin my book, just typical of my life.

I was the youngest of four children. My father always called me 'the babby' until the day he died, even though I was in my forties. I was born in 1952 to Ivy and Archibald Kelsey. I had two older sisters and one older brother and, yes, I was spoiled. My father was an electrician by trade and had his own business as an electrical contractor. He also loved sea fishing and built two cabin cruisers which, of course, he named after me. They were moored in Anglesey on the Menai Straits but sadly I never went on either of them. Water and I just don't mix, I'm terrified of it. I'll only paddle if I have my wellies on. I couldn't swim and for some reason I was always ill when it came to my swimming lessons at school.

My family were quite well off. We lived in a detached house in West Vale, Little Neston on the Wirral until I was about ten years old. Quite a few housing estates have been built since in West Vale but before that there used to be a big quarry there. It was enormous and men on motorbikes used to ride up and down the quarry walls and do stunts. I remember my brother Rod often taking me there, it was SO EXCITING to watch them.

Later on, we moved into a massive detached house my dad had built in one acre of gardens in Sandy Lane, Little Neston. There were no other houses around then, all you could see for miles around were fields. They named it Thicket Ford, No 1 Sandy Lane. Over time another ten houses were built on Sandy Lane but our house remained No. 1 even though there were three houses before ours. We had a massive driveway and large gardens and Dad kept his boats by the garages. Everyone thought we were super rich or film stars! The people we grew up with in Neston still talk about it.

When I was younger I had three different birthdays in my life. Who else has three birthdays! This says it all really doesn't it. Anyway, when I was little I used to have my birthday parties on 27th March as that was the date Mum told me my birthday was and it always annoyed me as it was near Easter. When my friends came over to my house my birthday presents were always Easter eggs. I'm not that fond of chocolate and I used to hate it. I'd think to myself 'oh no, not another Easter egg' and wonder why I couldn't have a nice toy for a change. When I got older I realised my birthday wasn't the 27th March and Mum told me it was 23rd March. So then I used to have my birthday parties on 23rd March until when I was older I checked my birth certificate and found out my actual birthday was 22nd March. I celebrate my birthday now on 22nd March, but my children always say to me year after year what day are you having your birthday this year Mum? I must be the only person in the world who can have their birthday every Friday or on the Saturday each year or whenever I choose to have it. I was so annoyed because there was never any need to have my birthday near

Easter on 27th and this is why I'm terrible at remembering dates. And there won't be many dates mentioned in this book for that reason. Two of my children have their birthdays on the 20 something of the month and I get mixed up with the dates even now. I blame my Mum.

When I was four and a half years old I started to attend Thornton Hough primary school like my sisters and brother before me. My Dad also went to this school. He was one of a large family of six brothers and a younger sister (whom I was named after). His family owned a big farm in Thornton Hough, a small hamlet on the Wirral. When the 2nd World War started five of the brothers went away to war, my Dad joined the RAF and was based in Canada. Oh, just thought I'd mention I wasn't born until after the war had finished by the way! Dad's family farm was called Yew Tree Farm in Thornton Hough and it still looks the same to this day. Dad would often take Rod and I to see Uncle Charlie who had taken the farm over after grandad had died. Another brother, Uncle Ernie also lived on the farm.

My eccentric Uncle Ernie was a gunsmith by trade. He made and sold guns to rich people, celebrities, the gentry (or toffs as Dad and he called them!) from all over the world for when they went to country estate shoots and for clay pigeon shooting. I think it was for that anyway? Each gun was worth a small fortune and he had them all lined up along the walls of his shed on the farm. He told us Sean Connery had bought guns from him. Uncle Ernie loved his guns so much he ended up living in his shed with them! I did say he was eccentric. Well that's life, it's never dull!

Whenever Dad took us to the farm I used to love playing with the pigs even though their sties were so smelly. Poor Rod always ended up getting chased by the geese. What is was about Rod I don't know but a couple of geese always used to chase after him down the fields; ah, poor Rod! I bet he's never forgotten those geese.

There is a lovely old church there in Thornton Hough and Dad was laid to rest there, also my baby grandson Jayki was later laid to rest there very near to Dad's grave. When Mum died a few years ago, she was also by Jayki and Dad. The church has a tall spire and Dad often told me about the time when he was a boy and he climbed this spire and the local bobby was called out and dad got into so much trouble. I always go inside the church and say a prayer whenever I am visiting the graves, because I know Mum would want me to. On one such visit I got locked inside the church. I tried each and every way to open the door but all in vain. After about fifteen minutes I was thinking calmly about how I would get out. After twenty-five minutes and no sign of anyone I started to panic. Then, lo and behold, the door magically opened, miracle or not I was so relieved. Every time I go in now I never 'SHUT THAT DOOR".

When I was about six years old I remember walking through a park in Neston, it was a short-cut and Mum took me through it whenever we went shopping. Everyone walked backwards and forwards through it to get to Neston shops. It had a tennis court, bowling green and two gated gardens which had winding paths, little bridges and streams and lots of beautiful plants and flowers. It was so magical. After shopping, Mum used to buy us a fresh cream cake each and we always went into one of the gardens and sat and enjoyed our cakes. One particular day Mum met up with a friend of hers and we all walked through the park with me running ahead when I saw a man with a gun in his hand pointing it at me. I was terrified. I ran back to Mum and told her and she told me not to be so silly. We carried on our way with no further incidents. It was only years later that I realised it wasn't a gun but a man exposing himself to me – what a weirdo.

I used to set off for school with my long hair in two neat plaits, a ribbon carefully tied in a bow on each, a school tie round my neck and my white socks neatly pulled up. I also used to wear a red beret – until the day I posted it into the village letter box walking home with my friend! I've no idea why I did it! On my way home from school I would be unrecognisable with one or both plaits undone and the ribbons missing, no tie, my top button undone on my blouse and my now grubby socks rolled down. I looked as though I'd been dragged through a hedge backwards!

I can remember learning to knit at school. We had to knit mittens with four needles. For some reason I just couldn't get the hang of it so some of my friends did my knitting for me whilst I helped them by threading their needles in our sewing lessons. I remember getting shouted at for always forgetting (on purpose) to bring my knitting into school. God, how I hated those red mittens. PS They never got finished!

Our class teacher was called Miss Torade. She was a small, elderly lady with a crippled foot which meant she had to wear a big built-up boot on one foot. She was very strict indeed and if anyone was naughty they would be made to stand in front of the class and she would slap them with a ruler, punishment which is unthinkable these days but quite common back then.

We all used to get the bus to school and quite often we would visit the little village sweet shop after school and spend all our bus fare on sweets. This meant we would then have to walk the five miles home to Neston!

When it was time for our school reports to be sent home, I always used to alter my grades and then tell my parents the teacher had a wobbly pen! I don't recall them ever questioning this!

Sadly, I failed my 11 plus exam. I say sadly as Mum and Dad wanted me to go to grammar school like my two sisters before me. Instead, I went to Neston Secondary School and have lots of happy memories of those days. Except for the maths lessons! I was awful at maths but our teacher, who was Welsh, was another very strict teacher and I was always too scared to tell him when I didn't understand something, so I used to look out of the window day dreaming until his loud voice would interrupt my thoughts. "KELSEY" he would shout at me. I will always remember his nose. It was deep red and purple and bulbous and the other kids used to say it was because he picked it and when anyone had their heads down concentrating on their work, he would pick his noise and flick it at them. I doubt this was true, but at the time I was always worried in case it happened to me. I remember his name but think I'd better not reveal it to protect his identity even though he's probably been dead years, poor man.

Not long after I started Neston Secondary School, a boy in my class called Gordon wrote me a sweet love letter (my first!) asking me if I would go out with him. I did quite like him, but I was very shy so didn't pluck up the courage to speak to him. Later on, he used to walk me home from school. He never kissed me but kept on sending me these lovely little love letters and buying me chocolates. Years later, when I was married to Mick, I went into a bank in Ellesmere Port and saw that Gordon was one of the cashiers there. We didn't speak but what a small world it is!

Every year, on the first Thursday in June, the fair comes to Neston and stays until the following Monday morning. On the Thursday there's a big procession called the 'Ladies Day Walk'. Anyone can join in, people wear pretty dresses and carry staffs of flowers. There is always a band and when I was little there used to be a little monkey dressed in a suit that you could hold and have your photo taken with. The fair is still going now and recently celebrated it's centenary, a lovely old Neston tradition that I have very fond memories of.

As I got older, I used to go to the fair with my friends as many nights as we could. It was an occasion to get all dressed up and I remember one year I wore a lovely brown patterned silky mini-dress with long, lacy sleeves that were wide at the wrist. I thought I was the bees knees in it, I loved it. Our favourite ride was the waltzers, which I still love to this day. We all hoped to get pushed around by the men operating the ride as it was a sort of ritual that if you got pushed for the duration of ride you were very popular and everyone would look at you. We also liked going to the fair to meet nice looking boys from the neighbouring towns and villages!

One time at the fair I met a boy a boy on a scooter. He was a mod, and his scooter was covered in mirrors and furs – this was in the days of mods and rockers. He was from Heswall and the rockers in Neston didn't like the mods and especially mods from Heswall for some reason. He asked me if I would like a ride on his scooter around the park in Neston. I was a bit scared at first, especially going around corners, but quite enjoyed the experience. After the ride he gave me my first proper kiss to say goodbye and off he rode into the sunset. Years and years later, when I was married to my second husband and had two more children, I lived in Heswall. This boy still lived in Heswall and I regularly had to walk past his house. He was married with children and my youngest son was in the same class as his son. I often wondered if he remembered me and that kiss. He still looks the same as he did all those years ago. What a strange coincidence. How we all cried the following Monday morning in school as we watched all the fairground lorries leaving Neston for another year.

My parents were quite old when I was born so I never met my grandparents and never saw any photographs of them. I used to constantly wonder what they looked like as my siblings all had grey or blue eyes. I always felt the odd one out as I was a lot darker with dark brown eyes. People used to say to Mum that I was a proper Kelsey in looks, my Dad's side of the family. I honestly thought at that time that I was adopted! There didn't seem to be any baby or toddler photos of me and, when I mentioned this to her, she pointed to a couple of baby photos on the wall and told me they were of me when I knew they were photos of my sisters. How I longed to see photos of my grandparents to see if they had my dark looks. Years later when I had become psychic, I remember asking myself repeatedly who I looked like. That night my grandmother, Janet, appeared to me in a dream saying to me over and over again "you look like me, you look like me". I would still love to see a photo of her, oh well never mind that's life.

My two older sisters started dating rich men from wealthy families and if my Dad was in the garden when my sister's boyfriend called she pretended Dad was the gardener as he always wore overalls. He wasn't a man who liked to get dressed up and there was always tension in the house if he had to wear a suit.

He was a very strict older Dad and had old fashioned values. My two older sisters were always getting into trouble with Dad as they were growing up. They had to be in the house by 9 pm every night even when they were eighteen or nineteen years old. My poor brother Rodney was often chased down the garden by Dad with his belt in his hand. I remember Rod often being locked out of the house and having to spend the night in the greenhouse.

One sister, Pauline, went to the exclusive Lucy Clayton Modelling School in London, paid for courtesy of a rich boyfriend. My older sister Janet had the strictest treatment of all. When she was meeting her boyfriend Mike (Dad called him 'the Cowboy') from a very well to do family and whom she later married, I had to run up the lane to warn her Dad was in and not to bring Mike home. Mum did what she could to calm the situation but in those days it was a different world.

By the time my sisters were married and had homes of their own, I had grown very close to Rod who was still living at home. Even though he was five years older than me I would never go to bed until Rod went to bed. Poor Rodney had to go to bed at the same time as his younger sister and once in bed I constantly shouted "goodnight Rod" over and over again. I think this was maybe when I first started with my OCD. I wouldn't go to sleep until he answered me time after time. Also, when Rod's mates called round for him I would scream my head off until Mum made him take me with him. We went fishing – Rodney fished, and I collected the wild flowers and looked at the rabbits Rod pointed out to me. I loved these times with him but I know his mates used to get fed up having to take me with them.

Later on, the tables sort of turned on Rodney and me. Instead of me continually shouting goodnight to him at night, he used to always ask me before he went out if he looked nice. Did his shirt go with his trousers, etc. Rodney was always very nice looking with trendy long hair and I'll never forget him wearing bright red tartan trousers which were very fashionable at the time. My Dad used to go mad when he saw Rodney wearing them, it was a nightmare at home when that happened, but Rod always waited for me to give my opinion on his outfit and if I said something didn't look right he would immediately change it. I always used to wear Ben Sherman shirts. There used to be a Ben Sherman shop in Birkenhead where I bought all my shirts from. They were the height of fashion at the time and I remember having a lovely cream and brown shirt which I used to wear with dazzling white trousers. Quite often Rodney used to borrow this shirt too. What fun we had in those days, hey Rod!

When I was about fourteen I started going out and about with a very good friend of mine called Lynne. We used to get the bus to Liverpool and go clothes shopping together. We loved shopping in Chelsea Girl and then we would go for a Chinese meal. I felt so grown up. I was really into the fashion and had my own style even at that age. I wanted to wear clothes other girls my age weren't into. Lynne and I used to get all dressed up in our trendiest gear and go to Parkgate on a Sunday afternoon and walk along the front. It used to be buzzing with posh sports cars and hunky men and everyone would beep their horns as we walked by. We would go into a little café on the front and have a pot of tea and a crumpet. It made Sundays so memorable to be part of this exciting scene.

My Dad wanted me to join Parkgate Tennis Club like my sisters before me, hoping I would meet some nice wealthy boys. But not me, I wasn't interested. My sisters invited me to join them and their boyfriends ice skating on a pond in one of their gardens, hoping I would like one of their younger brothers. But that wasn't for me either. Instead I started going out to clubs in Liverpool and New Brighton.

In a club in New Brighton I met a tall, dark and handsome lad called Phil who was there with his best friend and his girlfriend. I didn't make any arrangements to meet him again but one day in my lunch break from work I popped out for a walk and as I went past Hamilton Square station I bumped into Phil. I was very shy in those days and I looked up at him in adoration. We chatted for a short time until I had to get back to work. Another audio typist called Carole came up to me in work and asked who the gorgeous bloke was she had seen me chatting to at the station. I was so engrossed talking to Phil I hadn't even seen her walk past! I went out with Phil and his friends a few times. I must admit he did look after me but soon he started getting me into trouble by making me stay out all night. I'm afraid to say that Phil was also a bad boy. I had no no idea until someone who knew him warned me about him and told me that he had been to borstal. The relationship ended when he was sent to borstal again and sent me a letter from there. Mum found it and went mad with me. Luckily, she didn't tell Dad.

I was now ready to start going out clubbing in Liverpool. Some of the boys we met there used to give us lifts back home to Neston (which they thought was in Wales). We used to admire the cars they were in and it was only afterwards we found out that the cars they were driving were actually stolen. More often than not the boys would appear to be really kind and polite only for me to find out later that they had been in trouble with the police. Little did I know then that I was already on course to meet, date and marry the biggest bad boy of them all!

On some of my nights out in Liverpool in my early teens (this is something you should never do nowadays) we used to hitch a lift home. I'll never forget it, taxis were out of the question and everyone used to hitch a ride home. I always made sure I sat in the back next to the door so I could jump out if need be. There have been many times when I've had to jump out of that door when the car was moving. How irresponsible I was, I can't believe some of the things I did then looking back.

Another time my brother Rod came home late after going to Chester races. He'd won a lot of money but because he was very drunk Dad went mad with him. I went downstairs into the kitchen and saw money all over the floor - Rodney's winnings. I helped Mum pick it all up and guiltily slipped a £10 note into my bra! Afterwards I felt bad about it, I've never told Rodney to this day, but I went to Liverpool with my stolen £10 note and bought two dresses from Miss Selfridge with it. I still remember one of the dresses. It was a gorgeous, baby blue, Grecian style mini dress.

I stayed on at school for an extra year to take a commercial course and left school at sixteen qualified as an audio typist. I gave up the shorthand, I didn't like it and couldn't get my head round it and went for an interview for an audio typist at Littlewood Pools in Canning Street, Birkenhead. I'll never forget the interview. My Mum came with me and we were both sat in a room waiting for me to be called in for interview and all the latest pop songs were being played loudly over the loud speaker. Mum said with a sarcastic smile on her face ' what a nice place this would be to work with all the pop music playing' but I realised later that that only happened in the summer when there was no football on. It helped the girls get through their work without getting bored. I initially thought there would be lots of men working there but I was dead wrong, the place was full of women checking the pools coupons. I loved working there though and stayed there up until I was six months pregnant with Michael.

Two of the other audio typists, Kathy and Jenny, were from Heswall and used to tell me about all the places they used to go to there on nights out. There was also another girl also called Jenny who was also a pools clerk and from Heswall and every time the horn went off to indicate our breaks we always enjoyed our cups of tea together. These girls were a couple of years older than me and they took it upon themselves to mother me. I remember when I had the nits they took me down to the toilets and combed the nits out of my hair on one of our breaks. We had to answer every single letter or late coupons that arrived, we had to type out the mistakes many people who entered the Pools made or they were expecting to get some winnings and due to the weather or post they had arrived too late to be entered into the competition. I often remember a couple of my friends who were also typists who worked in offices, thinking they had been busy if they had had to type ten letters a day, we had thousands and each one had to be replied to. At Christmas time as well as our desks piled up with letters to answer we also had to pile them up on chairs and on the floor next to us, but

I loved it there. We used to get some bitchiness as you would expect from hundreds of girls. Some pools girls looked at you if you looked into a mirror and thought you were it. Writing this today I met Jenny 2 from Littlewoods and she told me that she had a coffee with Kathy and they had a good reminisce about Littlewoods. Life is so full of coincidences. When I bumped into Jenny 2 the other day she reminded me about Littlewoods Pools Beauty Competition that was held once. I didn't enter because all the girls had to be the same height for some reason. Jenny 2 didn't win it, but she told me about the purple dresses that they all had to wear. The girl who won it, God I don't remember her name now, was also a pools clerk and do you know what since I married my second husband and moved to Heswall I see her every time I shop in Heswall , she's a cashier. I've never mentioned I worked at Littlewoods to her but maybe one day I'll say something to her. Little did I know in later life I would also be living in Heswall and I would often bump into them in Tesco or around the village on a regular basis. Another big coincidence of how my past life keeps on entering this life. Coincidence I don't know or is it fate? Never mind, hey!

Chapter Two: I Meet Mick

One Wednesday night when I was about seventeen years old an old school friend of mine called Linda asked me to go out with her to a pub in Great Sutton called The Bull. There was a live group playing that night that she particularly wanted to see. I went along with her and had just walked in and sat down at a table when these two men walked in. One had a cream suit on with a handkerchief in his pocket and an open-necked shirt. He was tall, dark and handsome with a little Mexican moustache and long sideburns. I thought he was so handsome with his beautiful, big slanted deep brown eyes framed by long, thick eyelashes. I think I fell for him the moment I set eyes on him (our son Mike also inherited those eyes). He had a very confident, self-assured look that made you want to look at him. They had both also noticed us at about the same time. For some reason at that time I thought my side profile was my best feature, so every time Mick looked over at me I turned my head away from him, so he could see my profile!

After about ten minutes they walked over to us and introduced themselves. Mick was with his best friend John (who later married Linda and they had a child together). They bought drinks for us - my favourite drink at the time was Cherry B and cider - and stayed with us listening to the group and dancing. I loved the way Mick spoke. He had a Cockney accent which he still has to this day and perfect manners. At the end of the evening we exchanged phone numbers and Mick and John drove us both home to Neston.

It was Mick driving that first time. He opened the car door for me to get in and when we stopped he got out and opened my door for me to get out – the perfect gentleman! We had a bit of a snog and made arrangements for us all to meet up in a couple of nights time. This time they took us to a club in Ellesmere Port which was called the Waverley. I had never been there before and I remember thinking it was a huge place. Mick wore a pale brown suit with a cream open neck shirt. He looked so handsome and we had a fab night together. We danced and flirted the night away until the club closed. Mick was the most amazing dancer I have ever seen. I think he may have invented break dancing! He used to get down on the floor with his hand supporting him and had the most amazing dance moves. Everyone used to stop dancing and form a circle around him, all clapping.

A few nights later we all went out together again. This time Mick took us to a new pub in Great Sutton which became the 'in' place to go and be seen. Quite often Mick would take me out for a Chinese meal at the end of the night. Our favourite Chinese restaurant was near the docks in Ellesmere Port in quite a rough area but the food was amazing, I have never had a Chinese meal since to rival it. The only drawback was that the restaurant had a pub attached to it which stayed open all night, so everyone used to have a few too many drinks and then fights would break out. Word always got to Mick that a fight was starting and, although he never started any fights himself, he couldn't resist joining in. He always liked to even the numbers up so each side was equal and he always took the side of the underdog. He would make sure I was out of harm's way in a taxi going home and quite often I would turn around and could just make Mick out at the bottom of a pile of brawling men. In those days I think Mick just liked to let off steam. There were never any knives or guns and no one was drugged up. The most anyone would end up with would be a black eye or a broken nose – unlike today.

Over the years people have commented on how quickly I eat my food. Well, I blame Mick. We would never order a starter or pudding and I would tuck into my food as soon as it arrived in case a fight broke out and Mick would send me home! It happened quite often when we were out enjoying a meal and I tried to make sure I ate quickly enough to finish it before the bother started!

I also remember thinking I had been locked in the loo at this restaurant and screamed out for Mick to get me out. The next moment he had kicked the door open and dragged me out. I found out later I should have pushed the door open instead of pulling it. Mick was always my hero in those days. We all enjoyed some great nights out in the various pubs and clubs Mick took us to. He always acted like a gentleman towards me.

It wasn't long before Mick took me home to meet his Mum and Dad and little brother Mark. Mick's older brother John was serving in the Royal Navy and he was often away at sea, so we didn't see much of him. His Mum, Eira, was very good looking and his Dad Joe was a painter and decorator. He also had a nan and grandad living just a few doors away. Quite often Mick and I would babysit his brother Mark who was still at primary school. We would all watch films together and then have a takeaway. Mark also liked to get the crayons out and I spent many hours with Mark helping him to colour in his book. Sometimes when I was staying there and everyone had gone out to work I used to cook Mark's lunch for him when he came home from school at dinner time. I don't think I ever cooked him anything except tomato soup. I think it was his favourite meal – I hope it was as that's all he ever got! He was a lovely little boy, very well-mannered like the rest of the family. When he grew up he followed in his big brother John's footsteps and joined the Royal Navy too.

After we had been dating for several months we suddenly stopped seeing each other for about eight weeks. I remember thinking it was strange at the time that I hadn't heard from Mick and wondered if anything was wrong. Mick then got back in touch and we resumed our relationship. A friend of Mick's who lived near him came over to me one day while I was waiting for him and told me that Mick had been in Risley Remand Centre and that I should think twice about dating him. Did I take the advice – no, not me!

In the meantime, my friend Linda had moved into a flat with three other people in a big, old house in Bromborough just opposite the police station. The house was massive with a large basement where some of the boys had a flat with all the walls painted black, ideal for holding raves in. It was the place to party at that time. Occasionally I stayed with Linda if we had been out together and Mick would often pick me up from the flat in the morning. Eventually, I moved into the flat with Linda and it was in this flat that Mick and I first slept together. He often stayed over after that. I'll never forget the first time I saw Mick naked, I was so embarrassed, I had never seen a naked man before (I was very innocent then). I can remember thinking he had a very hairy chest and gradually came to love his amazing, muscular body.

The old house had a big overgrown garden where lots of feral cats lived. Our flat shared a communal lounge and kitchen with another couple who used to let the cats inside and the place started to smell badly. I blamed the cats for another unpleasant episode that happened during my stay there but later realised the cats were infested with fleas, not lice.

The first time I became aware I had head lice was when I had gone shopping to Liverpool with my Mum. She was walking slightly in front of me and when she turned around to see where I was she found me standing in the middle of the floor scratching my head like mad. She shouted "Irene what on earth are you doing" but my head was so itchy I couldn't stop. After a while it became apparent we were all infected with nits – except Mick. I had long hair and when I had the nits Mick went to the chemist and bought me a special shampoo to get rid of them. That night he put newspaper on the floor and combed the nits out of my hair. I'll never forget the sound of them landing on the newspaper – ugh! I can still remember feeling the eggs stuck to the strands of my hair and I used to get my nails and pull them all the way down until they dropped off. I think that's when I started picking at my skin – I still like a good pick now, especially cold sores!

At this time, I was beginning to feel a bit run down. I was the first person out to work in the morning and the last person to return to the flat in the evening. The kitchen was always dirty with soiled dishes and takeaway trays and I had to wash and clean up before I could cook my own tea. This was beginning to get me down and Mick had a word with the other couple who shared our kitchen who were responsible for the mess. If it was still dirty, Mick made a point of cleaning everywhere before I got in so that I would find everything spick and span. Another really sweet thing Mick used to do was to leave little notes saying 'I love you' in a bag of sugar or under my pillow or some other unexpected place! It was always a lovely surprise when I found them.

By now, Mick was spending a couple of nights at a time with me in the flat. I noticed that him and John came and went at unusual times during the night and early morning. Mick would never tell me what they were doing but I realise now they were up to no good. There was always a lot of whispering going on between them which would stop whenever I walked in. One day Mick and, I think, John had to go to court for something that had happened previously. He wasn't expecting to come home after the court appearance and I found it so stressful not knowing if he would be coming back to me that evening or staying at one of her Majesty's establishments. Mick's Mum told me she would be cooking his favourite meal for him, steak and onion pie, if he came home that night. Finally, to our relief he did come home. Apparently, he had a lenient judge who was in a particularly good mood that day. I've been told since that this does happen in some court cases even to this day.

Around this time my OCD got worse. I used to have to do certain things in the same order morning and night. I started touching the ornaments next to my bed one after the other for five times. If Mick asked me what I was doing, or I was interrupted, I would have to start the whole procedure over again.

Ten months after moving into the flat I found out I was pregnant. I had a feeling I was pregnant before I visited the doctor. I remember a gypsy knocking on the door of the flat one day and asking me if I wanted to buy some lavender. She told me she could see me looking over a crib at a baby boy and he would bring me a lot of luck – Mike! I'm still waiting for the good luck to happen. Well, never mind.

Mick was over the moon at the news. He couldn't wait to be a dad. Mick's parents were pleased too and thought that perhaps now Mick would settle down and keep out of trouble. I'm afraid that didn't happen though. Mick was still spending part of the week with me in the flat and the rest of the time with his parents. We had started collecting things for our bottom drawer – things like pans, brushes, towels etc. I remember one day I was annoyed with Mick for coming home late one night so I locked him out of the flat. The flat was on the top floor of the building and the bedroom window looked down on the driveway. Mick was standing beneath the window pleading with me to open the door. I was so mad with him I refused to and instead opened the window and threw out all the bottom drawer items we'd spent ages collecting. Out they all went one after the other, even the brushes went, but I think it was the toaster that hit him on the side of his head! In the end he gave up and went off to spend the night elsewhere. It's only now when I'm reminiscing thinking 'my God, that could have been a scene from his movie!' Oh, I do hope I didn't start him off throwing objects around in prison – oh dear, sorry Mick!

The following day we had both had time to calm down a bit. When I walked into the hall in the morning I noticed a piece of paper had been pushed through the letter box. It had Mick's writing on it and it was a poem telling me how much he loved me and saying he wanted to marry me. It was so romantic, it brought tears to my eyes! I couldn't wait to see him and say 'yes, I would love to be his wife'. I was so happy even though I was pregnant because I knew we both loved each other. Mick didn't buy me an engagement ring but went out and bought my wedding ring instead. For some reason I always seem to miss out on getting engagement rings. Oh well, never mind, there's still time I hope!

After we had kissed and made up we went to Chester Registry Office to book our wedding. We booked it for the beginning of January and I went out and bought a gorgeous white mini dress with wide sleeves and a hood with white fur around it. Mick bought me a white bible to carry.

My pregnancy was starting to show a bit more now and I looked as though I had a football pushed up my jumper. I never plucked up the courage to tell my parents I was pregnant and my Mum thought I was getting fat because I was eating too much. Ah, poor Mum, bless her!

Mick now had a job as a builder's labourer in Ness and spent his day carry bricks up and down the ladder for the bricklayers. I used to pop round and see him at lunchtime on my days off work and take sandwiches for him. He loved the fact that I had taken the time to make something for him to eat and got a bus to where he was working. Later on, when we were married, Mick worked as an industrial painter. It was his job to climb up the very big chimneys at factories and paint them. I remember he did like all the climbing – this would come in very handy in his later life when he made rooftop protests!

When I was six months pregnant with Mike, I left my job at Littlewoods Pools. I was very sad to leave work as I loved my job and enjoyed the company of the girls I worked with in the Correspondence Department. One thing I wouldn't miss though was the lewd glances of some of the men whose job it was to move the empty crates of football coupons. We would have to keep going up and down the stairs to our desks and, as most of us wore mini-skirts, you could guarantee there would always be a man standing at the bottom of the stairs looking up our skirts.

Whenever the girls asked me what I wanted as a leaving present I asked them for things for the baby. There were blue romper suits, blue Babygros, blue cardigans – everything blue for a boy. I just knew the baby I was carrying was a boy. This was in the days before scans were available to determine the sex of a baby. On the day I left work they presented me with practically everything we would need for the baby – except for the pram. Mick always met me off the bus from work and on my leaving day he was amazed by all the beautiful presents we had been given. Everything came in very handy indeed after Mike arrived.

Another time during my pregnancy Mick arrived home with a white boxer dog. I can't remember its name now, but the poor dog started displaying all the symptoms of my pregnancy. Mick took it to the vets who told him he dog was having a phantom pregnancy to be like me!

Mick was always very well-mannered and courteous to me. During my pregnancy he made sure I had enough rest and fussed over me constantly. His mum Eira always cooked me liver and cabbage at least once a week, a nourishing meal for me and the baby growing inside me. I didn't have any crazy pregnancy cravings but I was always buying green grapes. I still love them now!

About a month before the wedding I noticed something strange was going on between Mick and John. I think they were conspiring to commit a crime. There was the usual whispering and awkward silences whenever I came in. I'm sure it was to do with a train, but Mick never discussed this other part of his life with me. I think John's girlfriend knew something about what was going on but I do remember at this time there seemed suddenly to be a lot of money around. They all had new shoes and I remember I had gone out and seen a lovely pair of soft leather, white, knee-high boots in a shop in Liverpool and desperately wanted them. I couldn't afford them at the time but Mick went out and bought them for me and I thought they would look lovely with my wedding dress. Ill-gotten gains or what, I'll never know but God I loved those boots. After I'd worn them a few times I remember painting them red, white and blue and putting union jacks all over them. Later on again I dyed them lime green.

We only had a very small wedding at Chester Registry office. I remember it being very, very cold on the day and snowing heavily. My sisters drove me from our family home in Neston to meet Mick and his parents in Chester. That old saying 'happy is the bride the sun shines on' must be true as it was snowing on our wedding day. Mick wore a lovely dark grey suit and looked really smart, as ever. He didn't have a wedding ring, but I had a white gold engraved ring which I loved. (Later on I pawned this much-loved ring for £3 at Birkenhead market in order to buy a handbag. I regret not going back to claim the ring, how stupid was I?)

My parents didn't come to our wedding. I don't think they thought a lot of Mick and certainly didn't want me to get married. They didn't know I was pregnant either – if they had known I don't know if they would have had a change of heart.

When we were taking our vows, we looked at each other and both burst out laughing and couldn't stop. We were unable to get our words out, the Registrar just kept repeating everything until we eventual managed to say them. It was so embarrassing, but we couldn't help it, all you could hear was our nervous laughter. After the ceremony was over we went to Mick's parent's house in Great Sutton, Ellesmere Port for food and some drinks. When my sisters left later Mick and I went to The Bull pub (where we had first met) for a couple of drinks. I can't really remember much more of our wedding day after that. I know we went back to Mick's parent's house where we would be living until the baby was born. Then we planned to get a council house in Ellesmere Port.

I don't have any photos of our wedding day. A few years after we married, during one of our rows, I cut up all the wedding photographs in a fit of temper and Mick then burnt them with his lighter. Oh well, never mind. I've lost count of all the times I've later regretted destroying them.

Chapter Three: Married Life

In the later stages of my pregnancy I had moved into Mick's parents' house in Bebington Road, Great Sutton. One Saturday evening in June about 7pm, I started getting contractions and went into labour. Mick was totally panic stricken and his Mum and Dad suggested he phone for an ambulance to take me into hospital for the birth. The hospital was Clatterbridge Maternity Hospital, an old red brick building set in the Cheshire countryside, which sadly no longer exists. I will always remember walking in from the ambulance through a small side door with Mick at my side carrying my little suitcase, all the time fussing over me and trying to reassure me. Mick was asked to wait outside the room while they admitted me and prepared me for the birth. This was in the days when, prior to the birth, the midwife shaved off your pubic hair and gave you an enema! I don't think that happens nowadays. I could hear Mick asking people walking past in the corridor outside if I was alright. Eventually I was moved onto the labour ward but poor Mick was frantic with worry as he wasn't allowed to be with me and didn't know what was going on. In those days you were not allowed to have anyone with you in the labour ward, even your husband, so Mick had to sit in the waiting room and wait … and wait…and wait. It was a very long labour, almost 24 hours, and I remember I had a student midwife with me the whole time who must have been really tired towards the end. Strangely enough for me, I was very calm and finally gave birth to a lovely baby boy, Michael, weighing in at 7lbs 8oz on 4th June.

When they let Mick come into the room to see me and the baby he was overcome with emotion and over the moon. Even newborn, it was clear Mike was the spitting image of his dad. Once Mick knew we were both ok, he went home to Great Sutton. It was the early hours of the following morning by this time and in his rush and panic Mick had left the house with no shoes on and no money in his pocket, so he walked all the way back to Great Sutton in his bare feet.

A few days after the birth I was moved from Clatterbridge to a maternity unit in Bromborough. In those days you were in hospital for a week or more with your first baby. When Mick came at visiting time, a doctor came over to talk to us. He asked if we had any coloured relations because Mike had a lot of purple bruise-like marks all over his body. No-one could understand what had caused them as the birth had been easy and I had been calm throughout it. The doctors thought that if we had non-white relatives the marks may have been uneven pigmentation on Mike's skin. When we told him no, he was at a loss to understand what had caused it. Later on, when Mick had overstayed the allocated visiting time, a specialist came over to speak to us. He told us he had worked in China and had seen a lot of Chinese babies born with similar marks on their bodies which eventually faded and then disappeared completely. Thankfully, this was the case with Mike but to be honest Mick and Mike have got the same deep brown slanted eyes so maybe there was a relation in the distant past who was Chinese.

A week after giving birth to Mike I was allowed to go home to Mick's parents' house in Great Sutton with the baby whom we called Michael Jonathon – Michael obviously after his dad and Jonathon after Mick's older brother who was in the Royal Navy. (Sadly, by the time Mike was christened it was many years later and Mick had already been in prison for about six years.) Mick picked us up from hospital in his car and proudly showed me the bedroom he'd decorated for us at his parents' house. Everything was newly painted and he had set up the crib for Mike next to our bed. It was covered in a lovely pale blue broderie anglais material in which all Mick's older cousins had slept in when they were babies. I remember my Mum cutting up her best cotton sheets and making cot and pram sheets for us. Mick was a very devoted dad to Mike. He took him out for long walks for miles in his pram. Sometimes we walked all the way from Great Sutton to Little Neston to visit Mum and Dad. Mike always pushed the pram – a big navy-blue Silver Cross pram, nothing like the prams these days. We used to walk through a little village with huge, mansion style houses set back behind high walls. Quite often Mike used to stop and climb up the walls and look over the top and look at the houses. I would ask him what he was looking at and he used to say he was looking at the gardens. I didn't realize then that he was probably sizing them up for some sort of crime, but I couldn't ever be sure, not even to this day. I just thought he wanted to look at the houses and gardens!

Quite often Mick would take us out to Chester for the day on the bus. We used to have a pushchair that you could fold up and whenever we got the bus Mick would carry the pushchair, Mike and any shopping we had. He would never let me carry anything. In those days when you got on the bus you had to fold your pram up, which was difficult as they were more cumbersome then. I was often on my own, carrying Mike, the pram and shopping and paying the driver my fare. Honestly, women don't know how easy they have it these days; just push the pram on the bus and everyone moves out of their seats to make it even easier for them. Oh well, never mind hey!

One of my favourite walks was back to Mum and Dad's house in Little Neston. It took about an hour of fairly fast walking to get there but I really enjoyed these visits. Although my parents did not attend my wedding, they loved Mike dearly and really spoiled him. Mum would always be at the window waiting for us and as soon as we arrived we would go straight into the kitchen where a pot of tea and a slice of homemade cake would be waiting for us on the long wooden table (I now have this table in my own kitchen). Dad would carry Mike out into the garden and Mum and I would have a nice chat.

On one of these visits, not long after Mike was born, an invitation had arrived in the post from a male friend of mine, whom Mike always referred to as 'one of your posh friends'. I was so excited because it would be the first time since being pregnant and having Mike that I would be able to go out and have some

fun and to drink my favourite drink of Cherry B and cider. Mick too was excited about going and so off we went to the party. We had only been there for
about two hours when Mick disappeared upstairs. When he came back down
he walked right up to me and then collapsed in a dead heap at my feet. We
couldn't wake him up. I was furious with him. Two of the men had to carry him
outside, still flat out, and take us home to Mick's parents' house in a white van.
I know his mum was angry with him but not as mad as I was! My first time out
in ages and Mick had to collapse and we had to go home early. I never, ever for-
gave him for that! It was years afterwards that I found out he had taken a purple
heart pill whilst upstairs, and also that everyone upstairs was walking around
naked in a drug infused daze! I have no idea if this was true or not – I certainly
never saw anything like that happening downstairs, but, sorry Mick, I did kick
you a few times when you were lying flat out on the floor! I was so angry with
you! I know you probably had no recollection of it and have never mentioned
that bit in your books when you talk about the party. Sorry Mick!

When Mike was a few weeks old, he started to get severe pains in
his stomach and he would draw his little legs up to his chest causing him to
cry and cry nonstop for a couple of hours every single night. It always started
at six o'clock at night for some reason; we just couldn't do anything to help
him or stop his crying. We all tried everything possible, nursing him, trying to
distract him from the pain, pushing him and rocking him in his pram, all to no
avail. Then, one day, Mick's dad Joe came in with a dummy he'd bought from
the chemist. We tried that and it did seem to help occasionally to a degree, but
thankfully Mike grew out of it and the doctor told us Mike was suffering from
colic – a regular occurrence in babies after their six o'clock feed brought on by
wind, although we did burp him after his feeds. Silence is golden – yes, they got
that dead right! Bliss!

While we were living with Mick's parents we put our name down with
the local authority for a council house. We used to visit Ellesmere Port Council's
offices every week to see if a house had become available for us. Even though
Mick's parents were really good to us, we were anxious to be on our own in our
own house.

Then one day when Mike was about six months old, we got the
long-awaited letter to say we had been given a house in nearby Little Sutton.
We couldn't wait to go and view it. It was a corner house in a large cul-de-sac
with a front, side and large back garden and a railway line that ran along the
rear perimeter fence. For a council house it had a big, private garden and we
were over-the-moon with it.! To celebrate, Mick asked his parents to babysit and
off we went that night to all the pubs we used to frequent when we were going
out with each other. Much later on that night we decided to park the car up
somewhere for a bit of a snog. Mick drove to the secluded Ness marshes not far
from a very old pub called The Harp and we parked up. By this time, it was well
past midnight and pitch black and we weren't really sure of our exact location

except that it was near a field close to the marshes. Anyway, after a couple of hours we decided we had better head for home. Mick started the car up but couldn't get it to move! The wheels just spun round churning up mud. Mick tried everything to get it to move; he put it in reverse which did move it a couple of inches but that was all. We had the car headlights on and all we could see was fields and marshland. Oh my God, we were stuck fast in mud on Ness marshes, miles from civilisation in the pitch black, in the early hours of the morning. Mick suggested we ring someone to try and tow us out. I rang my brother-in-law to see if he could help us but, because it was freezing cold and the middle of the night, he refused to come out.

As we saw it, we only had one other option open to us. Mick said we'd have to leave the car and try and find someone, somewhere to tow us out. So, we stepped out of the car, ughh, into mud, slime, cow dung, cow urine, every nasty substance you could think of, right up to our ankles. It was awful, our feet stuck with every footstep. Mick was frantic. He had a lovely suit on which he hadn't had long (he always had his suits made-to-measure). Mick never, ever wore jeans, not even for work. His suit trousers were covered in this stinking, black, gunky mud. I was laughing my head off, I couldn't stop laughing! Maybe if I'd had on my lovely white leather platform knee-high boots I definitely would not have been laughing either but luckily for me I was wearing a pair of shiny, stretch knee-high boots from which I could easily wash off all the slime and mud. Poor Mick, he had to throw his trousers away afterwards! They were too badly stained even after being cleaned. Oh, never mind Mick!

Anyway, we plodded slowly along, Mick moaning about his trousers, me laughing hysterically, until we eventually came to a farm. We walked up to the farmhouse and knocked on the door. Ah, the poor farmer, we woke him up and still he didn't mind helping us. He got on his tractor and took us back to where we thought Mick's car was and hauled it out of the mud. What a relief, by this time Mick was laughing about it too but he was always more careful after that where he parked up! He definitely learnt from his mistake that time, didn't you Mick! When we arrived back at Mick's parents' house, needless to say, they weren't very happy with Mick.

Not long afterwards Mick said that he wanted to take me out for a drink again, only locally this time, no driving involved. My Mum gave me some money to buy a new dress and off I went to my favourite shops in Liverpool, Chelsea Girl and Miss Selfridge, and bought a bright red and white polka dot, halter neck dress, which I thought would go great with my lovely soft, white leather knee high, platform boots. I was sooo excited. Mum and Dad offered to have Mike for the rest of the day as well as that night for me. So off I went back to Mick's house and when he came home from work I showed him the new dress. His reaction was not what I was expecting. He took one look at it and said it was far too provocative for me to wear now that I was married, and he got the scissors and proceeded to cut my beautiful dress up into tiny pieces. I was horrified, I hadn't seen this side of him before and obviously wasn't too happy about it. We had a massive row and I think this was the time when I got the scissors and cut up all our wedding photographs in retaliation. Mick then got his lighter out and burned the cut-up photographs. He got bathed and changed into one of his suits and went out to the pub leaving me fuming on my own. I then went to the off-licence and bought some Cherry Bs and cider and got drunk in our bedroom on my own- and I mean drunk! By the time Mick came back in I was slightly inebriated, shall I say, and Mick had to undress me and put me to bed! He was really not happy with me and I was really, really not happy with him either, so there!

I'm writing this whilst I'm on the bus on my way to work at Ann Summers. I've got my scarf wrapped around my face so that all you can see of me are my eyes and the top of my head. Yes, I have had a couple of double takes from some of the other passengers. One man came and sat by me - why me when there were plenty of empty seats – and asked me who I was hiding from, ha ha? 'The germs' I said. Oh well, never mind hey, needs must!

Chapter Four: My Jekyll and Hyde Husband

One Saturday morning, not long after we got the keys to our new home, we were so happy we decided to go into Ellesmere Port and buy some furniture on hire purchase. We bought all white furniture; we had a lovely round, white coffee table, a white wall unit with shelves where we put different coloured glass vases, a white chest of drawers with two wardrobes either side and a little dressing table in the middle. Oh, and we got an amazing tv! It was also white and had a round pedestal stand and a round top. It was very 'the thing' at the time. I wish I still had it today, it was ultra-modern and very much of its era. We bought a purple carpet and purple wall paper – we thought we were the bees knees! Paper flowers were the thing as well in those days. I found an enormous, black glass floor standing vase into which we put some giant paper flowers. The kitchen was small and Mick had painted it bright orange and I had covered all the walls in giant daisy stickers - It was all very sixties, all the rage at the time.
 I was very artistic and liked to buy different coloured tins of paint and paint flowers on the kitchen tiles and walls. One day I thought to myself oh how nice it would be if I painted our bath. Blue was the colour I was thinking of and I knew there was a big tin of turquoise paint in the cupboard under the stairs. Mick was out at work and Mike was sleeping so that's what I did – bright tur-quoise! Whether I had used the correct paint or not I'll never know but I thought it looked fab! Eventually Mick came home from work and, as usual, he went straight upstairs and jumped into the bath. I'd forgotten to tell him I'd painted the bath and it was still wet. Too late, he sat down in it and jumped straight back up. He started shouting and I ran up the stairs to see Mick covered all over in bright turquoise paint! |I couldn't stop laughing, it was hilarious! Well it wasn't my fault, he'd rushed upstairs before I'd had a chance to tell him I'd painted it, but I must say turquoise really suited his dark good looks! Well, never mind hey!

Another day I decided to decorate Mike's bedroom. I bought some rolls of wallpaper covered in little zebras and elephants. Now don't ask me how on earth I managed it but I put the paste onto the paper and papered the walls. It looked lovely! I was so pleased with my efforts. When Mick came home from work, I showed him how clever I'd been. He turned to me and said "Irene, you do know that the pattern has to match up, don't you?!" Oh no, I hadn't even thought about that. Never mind, little Mike never noticed.
We had a little front garden, a side garden and a large back garden which was all grass. At the bottom of the garden was a railway line – thank God they had stopped steam trains by then otherwise my washing would have been covered in smoke. Yeahh!

The side our house was joined up to belonged to another young couple who also had a baby boy or girl (I can't remember which but it was one of them!) and as time went on I often thought to myself that Mick and she were so very alike; she used to drink a lot and leave the baby with her husband and disappear until all hours then you'd hear her come in, shouting and swearing her head off at her husband. Her poor husband never rose to her abuse. I got the impression that he had had a much better upbringing and I thought that she should be with Mick and I should be with the husband. I never fancied him or anything (he wasn't my type), I loved Mick but I thought it strange that both of our partners were that way inclined in drink.

Living on the other side of us was another young couple who had a little girl a few months older than Mike. I never really became close friends with her, she was very friendly with another girl from somewhere on the estate, but I did have to knock on her door one day when Mick was at work because I'd just fed Mike in his high chair and couldn't lift him out as he was stuck fast in it. They came in and managed to free him for me. God knows how he became stuck, but I was in a right panic.

Much later, when Mick was away in prison, this same girl did a moonlight flit with her family and at the same time took a lot of our possessions with her (she had a key to our house). Vases, records, my carpet cleaner, amongst other things, all disappeared with her. That was a shock to my system. I never told Mick anything about it or anyone else for that matter. It was just another incident for me to deal with on my own at that time whilst Mick was away.

Mick used to cut the front lawn and big back garden with a scythe as the grass was very long and a conventional lawnmower wouldn't cut it. One day when we were visiting my parents, Mum gave us a lot of privet cuttings to plant around our front garden which would eventually grow into a nice thick hedge. Mick planted them and carefully tended them and I remember an old lady who lived a few doors down from us coming up to us whilst we were busy in the garden and saying to us how nice it was to see such a young couple making such an effort to make their garden look nice. On another occasion I remember Mick and I looking through our bedroom window onto our lovely, tidy garden and we both felt so proud of it.

At this time Mick was working for a firm called Ellis and Perry in Ellesmere Port as an industrial painter He had to climb all those high, round petrol storage tanks on industrial estates – something which enabled Mick to do those roof top protests later on in his life! He made nine of those protests. When he was at Broadmoor, I'll always remember one Saturday lunchtime I was watching the tv news with my parents and there was Mick on the prison roof protesting; what a shock it was! It hurt me to the bone seeing him on that roof. Dad tried to make light of it to stop me from getting too upset . Those memories will never leave me. Anyway, back to my story. They used to pick him up from home early every morning before I got up. When I came down later to get Mike's breakfast and make my own, I would often find little notes left by Mick in the tea caddy or the sugar pot saying 'I LOVE YOU'. How sweet was that. He could be so nice and romantic at times. Ahh! Another time I hadn't slept much because little Michael had been unwell and an old school friend of mine was coming round for lunch. I was feeling so tired and was worried that I hadn't cleaned the kitchen floor. Mick made me sit down and brought me a cup of tea. Then he got down on his hands and knees with a bowl of soapy water and a scrubbing brush and cleaned the kitchen floor for me! Ahhh!

I made my friend my special cottage pie, or was it called shepherds pie?. Oh well, it was my special recipe! Sorry if you want to know it – you will have to come round for lunch!

Mick used to do time work, getting paid for the work you do regardless of how long it took. Sometimes it took longer than expected and sometimes he would finish early; either way he got paid the same amount. On those early finishes Mick usually went for a drink to a little local social club and then went to the pub in the evening with his mates. This meant that he used to have a lot to drink on these occasions and the following morning he would be standing on the front door step swaying from side to side. I hated those times when Mick had had too much to drink because he became a different person – like a Jekyll and Hyde character. Without the alcohol you couldn't meet a nicer, kinder person than Mick but I definitely didn't like the other side of his character.

One day after Mick had finished work, he came home for his tea and afterwards suggested we go for a walk and pop in to see his mum and dad. So off we went. We arrived at his parent's house (they lived in Great Sutton), had a cup of tea then after about an hour Mick said he had to go and see a mate. He promised he wouldn't be too long because baby Mike was getting tired and we needed to get home and put him to bed. Anyway, one hour passed, then two, then three hours passed and still no sign of Mick. Mick's dad tried ringing around the local pubs and Mick's mates to see if anyone knew where he was but to no avail. No-one knew his whereabouts. I was getting more and more annoyed. Mick's parents were starting to worry, little Mike was getting tired and grouchy so in the end Mick's dad said he would take us both home. As Mick had the only door key with him, he said he'd have to break a window to get us inside. He broke the kitchen window and opened the back door. Poor man, he then had to set about making the window secure with some plywood he found in Mick's little garden shed. Believe me, when Mick turned up the following morning we had a massive row about it – and I mean a massive, massive row!

Following a row we usually had a few peaceful days together. We went for walks with Mike in his pram and trips into Chester and other pleasant outings when Mick was in his Dr Jeckyll persona.

Every Saturday and Sunday Mick used to carry Mike on his shoulders and walk up to the local newsagents. Mike used to love sitting on his dad's shoulders. Quite often on a Sunday Mick's friends would call round for him and he would go off for a few hours with them. Where they went and what they were up to I never knew, I'm glad to say! If he was up to no good I never knew as Mick would never tell me anything about what he was doing or planning, I think probably to protect me.

Mick was also very possessive with me. I remember one night we were going out for a meal. Mick went into a shop to buy some cigarettes whist I waited outside for him. A car went past me and the driver hooted the horn at me. Mick came running out shouting "who was that beeping the horn at you? He was furious and he took me straight back home – no meal, no evening out. I was so mad at him I went up to our bedroom and waited until I heard Mick shut the front door and walk up the path. Yes, he was only going out without me for a drink and leaving me at home! Oh dear, here I go again! I opened the bedroom window and started to throw some of Mick's treasured trendy clothes out of the window after him. He didn't even look back. I was expecting him to come back and pick his clothes up but, no, he carried on walking to the top of the road and was gone for a few hours. When he returned he never mentioned his clothes all over the front garden but I did notice that he had taken them to the dry cleaners afterwards. Oh dear me, it was becoming a habit this - me getting mad with Mick and throwing his things out of the window in anger. I really hope I didn't start Mick on the way to throwing things about like he has done in jail. Oh dear! Mick did have a downside though, he was very posessive. He would say to me you're a married woman now and shouldn't want to wear all your trendy clothes. At the time I used to wear leather and suede mini skirts and shorts which were the fashion then.

When Mike was a toddler I signed on with an employment agency as a typist and was offered a job in Rock Ferry working for a family business who made wooden pallets. They exported these to South Africa and other counties. I use to hate it when the phone rang because I could never understand what they were saying or their names which I always got wrong, really, really wrong! There was one other girl working there as a typist with me. She had been there a couple of years and was obviously the favoured employee with the female boss we both worked for. She couldn't do anything wrong, so if she made a typing mistake the boss would just Tippexed them out but if I made a mistake she would put a line through them and I had to retype everything. After I had been working there for a few weeks Mick's grandad died and I asked her for the day off to attend his funeral with Mick. She said I couldn't have the time off , what a surprise ,she was a lovely lady – not! I was furious so I decided to stay off anyway but not before I wrote a letter about her saying how nasty she was (and a bit more) and left it in my desk at work.

When I went back after the funeral the other girl told me the female boss had looked in my desk drawer and found the letter. She came into the office later that day and called me into her office and sacked me! She said we don't pay you to sit there looking pretty! What a b.....ch she was. Oh yes she didn't like me at all and I certainly didn't like her either. I went home after collecting Mike from nursery school and Mick said not to worry as it was obviously a case of favouritism and she was probably very jealous of me too. I would point out that the other three members of the family business were men and they were always really lovely towards me. Just thought I'd mention that!

Never dance with the devil, he will trip you up: Charlie Salvador

As time went on Mick quite often disappeared for days at a time. I had no idea where he was. It was when there was no mobile phones, you couldn't just ring someone to see where they were, so I used to push Mike in his pram all over the place trying to find him but I never did. When he eventually came home I would ask him where he had been and he would say that he had a very bad hangover and had to stay at his friends until he felt better and I believed him. Was he hungover or not? I'll never know the answer to that one!

One day when Mike was about two years old Mick came home from work and ran upstairs as usual to have a bath. When he was upstairs there was a knock on the door and when I answered it there were two women standing there on the step. They said they wanted to speak to Micky. One of the women looked older than the other and I thought at the time they may have been mother and daughter. I'm not being nasty but I thought they were quite rough looking. I shouted up to Mick that there were two women at the door wanting to speak to him and then went to make them a coffee in the kitchen. I then went into the lounge and saw Mick was in there on his own. I asked where the women were as I'd just made them a drink and in reply he said don't ever invite slags like that into my home again. He never explained who they were or what they wanted and nor did I ask him about them but I was very naïve back then.

One Xmas I was telling Mick about the stocking my mum always used to give me on Xmas morning. She would cut up a pair of her tights and fill them with sweets, a tangerine and some silver coins, etc. , something I have also done with my own children. This particular Xmas morning when I awoke, Mick had made a stocking for me. He'd put in an apple, an orange, chocolates and a lovely purple and lilac nightie and matching negligee! It was so trendy and I loved it. Mick could be so, so romantic and thoughtful at times, bless him! The last time I wore that negligee set was one of the worst times I can remember with Mick. He had gone missing again and I've only just recently found out that he had in fact gone into hiding, not long before his High Court appearance. It was about 2am in the morning and there was a loud knocking on the front door. I started walking down the stairs and shouted out "who is it?" thinking it may be Mick but, no, it was the police – about five of them looking for Mick. I couldn't bring myself to wear that negligee again after that experience. There's more about this raid in the next chapter.

Another time little Mike was sitting in his high chair watching children's tv whilst I was giving him his lunch. I remember it was "Sooty" that was on, Mike's favourite programme at the time. Mick came home from work having finished the job for that day and the news came on the tv. Mick said to me "you are going to see me on the news one day" and I got the most terrible feeling in my stomach as though someone had walked over my grave. At the time I thought Mick was just joking but in the future I would see his face on the television many, many times – to my distress.

Not long after this, Mick was working at a job somewhere near St

Helens. The police called around to the house and asked to speak to Mick. He'd not long got home and apparently he had been speeding and there was a little crash he'd said but he carried on and drove home. They wanted to see Mick's car as Mick denied it was him involved in the accident but Mick had already got rid of the car and so he was never charged. Where he'd hid the car I had no idea, I was just grateful that nothing more was said about the incident.

One time I remember really well, Mick had been out drinking all afternoon and evening. I'd laid the dining table for tea and Mick hadn't come home so I had mine then put Michael to bed. At about 5am in the morning I heard Mick outside struggling to open the door so I went down and opened it to find Mick on the step swaying from side to side, yes very, very drunk! He'd even knocked a milk bottle over. I let him in and went back to bed and left him to it. The next thing I heard was Mick shouting and loud bangs coming from the dining room. Wondering what the hell was going on I went back downstairs and had such a shock. Mick had thrown his dinner at the wall, the coffee table was upside down, cushions had gone flying everywhere and he was just about to throw a vase at the television screen! It was like a scene from a nightmare. I got him to put the vase down and helped him up to bed. The following morning I got up and just looked at the mess Mick had made. I left it exactly as it was until Mick came downstairs. He looked around and said "my God Irene what on earth possessed you to make all this mess?" He thought I'd done it! I said you did this – you, you, you. You came home in the early hours of the morning very drunk and trashed the place!" He never believed me, he thought it was me! He was in a state of shock and couldn't remember a thing about the night before. I'm sure he eventually forgot about it but I never did. Fancy blaming me! It never happened again though. It was getting nearer and nearer to his High Court appearance and maybe that was causing the heavy drinking. Little did we know what was around the corner. Oh well, never mind hey!

Chapter Five: Arrest and Remand

Friday the ?????, sorry can't remember the exact date, but I know it was a Friday because it was pay-day for Mick and he always used to go to the Chinese chippie in Gt Sutton to get us a takeaway for our tea. Mike and I were starving waiting for our meal. Five o'clock, six o'clock came and went still no sign of Mick. Then, at about 7.30 at night Mick's dad came round with our take-away. Apparently Mick had asked him to get it for us as Mick had something to do in Ellesmere Port. I was furious with him, I didn't want him to go out drinking all the time. It turned out that from that Friday night I would not see or hear from Mick for another fortnight. Where the hell was he and what was he up to now? I tried to carry on as normal for Michael's sake, I kept to our usual routine all the time wondering where Mick was. I locked the doors at night knowing that if Mick came home I would hear him outside.

Mike used to ask me where his daddy was. I used to say he was still at work, very busy, but he'd be home soon so not to worry. I never told anyone at all that Mick was missing especially not our parents. I kept them in the dark. Then, two weeks later at about 2.30am in the morning, there was a knock on the front door. I thought thank God Mick's home at last. I put on my purple neg-ligee on top of my nightie and walked down the stairs saying "who is it, who is it?" "Mick, Mick " came the reply so I opened the door and about five policemen came in. One policeman stayed with me and the other four rushed upstairs. I asked them what was happening, what they wanted, and they said they were looking for Mick. I can't remember if they showed me a search warrant or not, I was up in the air not knowing what the hell was happening. The policeman who stayed with me was actually quite nice. He told me that he used to go to school with Mick. As he looked around the lounge he said that at least Mick had given me a nice home. I know I replied, we got most of it on HP. Thirty minutes later the other policemen came downstairs empty handed and they all left. I went upstairs to check if Mike was still asleep in his room and found him sitting up in his bed crying and asking me what those men wanted. I told him that one of them used to live in the house before us and had lost something he was looking for and his friends had come along to help him look. God love him, he was only a baby and didn't understand.

The next day Mick still hadn't turned up so I took Mike to a toy shop in Little Sutton and bought him a little bright red lorry to play with. He still remem-bers that little lorry and the night of the police raid even now after 48 years. I rang my mum from the telephone box nearby and asked her if we could come and stay for a few days. My parents came round to our house later that day to pick us up and apparently my dad said to mum he couldn't believe how messy I was – have you seen the mess , everything thrown on the floor and drawers open with stuff hanging out? It wasn't my mess it was the police from the raid. I couldn't bring myself to tidy up afterwards. They said they were looking for Mick but they wouldn't find him in the cupboards and drawers, would they?

Never eat a raw onion, it's bound to end in tears: Charlie Salvador

What exactly they were looking for I have no idea whatsoever.

A couple of days later I had made arrangements with my friend Kathy from Heswall to go and visit her with Mike. She was dying to see Michael and she hadn't long lost her mother so I didn't want to cancel the visit. I hadn't told Kathy or anyone else what had happened. She had given me instructions on how to get to Heswall and which buses to catch from Ellesmere Port. I got off at the wrong bus stop on the first bus and was then completely lost. I had ended up just outside Bromborough somewhere I hadn't been before. Mike was getting fed up so I took him to a big supermarket nearby to get him some sweets. As soon as I came out I realised I had lost my purse. I had to ask a woman to look after Mike while I rushed back inside to find my purse. I was in a right panic and couldn't find my purse anywhere. It was terrible – all my money was in that purse, how on earth was I going to get us both back home. My anxiety had kicked in big time. I was crying my eyes out as I ran back to the woman looking after Mike and, God bless her, she gave me £4 of her own money to get the bus back home and she also waited with me for half an hour for the bus to come and take me back to Ellesmere Port. She was definitely my angel that day! Back home I carried on alone for the next few days trying to stop myself from panicking and all the time wishing Mick would come back home to us. I kept telling myself over and over not to worry, everything would be alright once Mick got home. He never did.

Later that day Mick's dad Joe came round to see me with some bad news for me. He told me that Mick had been arrested and was being kept in the cells at Ellesmere Port police station. He had been asking to see me. OMG I was sick to my stomach. I remember going down lots of steps at the police station and then there was Mick in a tiny little box cell. He kept saying over and over again I'm sorry Irene, I'm so sorry Irene. I love you and I love Mike. I'm so sorry. It was a nightmare I would never wake up from.

The next time I was to see Mick was when he was on remand in Walton jail. Mick's mum, Mike and I went to see him. My first impression of the waiting room there was that it was like a dungeon in a castle. The walls were made out of stone with a long wooden bench along the side. It was a very scary place. From there we all went into a large canteen like room which had little tables in it. Once we were seated they let the prisoners come in and sit with their visitors. We were allowed to buy tea and pop and snacks for the children. I'm a great tea drinker – there's nothing better than a nice cup of tea! – so I thought to myself oh it's not too bad in here is it? You can buy tea and refreshments – just how naïve was I! Mick apologised again and again to me, telling me he loved us both and not to worry as it wouldn't be long before we'd all be back home again together. I had hope – it was what we were all depending on. When it was time to leave at the end of the visit and Mick was whisked away, Mike ran after him crying, Daddy! Daddy! It was heartbreaking for all of us. I was devastated.

Chapter Six: Prison Wife

I woke up very early in the morning with the sickest feeling in my stomach. Why do I feel like this? Why don't I want to open my eyes and face the day? Ohhh, I remember now - it was Judgement Day the 7th October 1974. I remember that day as if it was only yesterday. It was one of the most horrific days of my life. It was the day Mick was going to be sentenced at Chester Crown Court. I can't face this, I just can't I said to myself – but from somewhere I got the strength to get out of bed and get Michael and myself ready to get the bus to Chester and meet Mick's mum Eira and his aunty Eileen. Every single minute of that journey I was feeling devastated. I hoped I would never have to live through a day like that again. First impressions of the Court reminded me of an old castle. As we walked through the court grounds we saw a black mariah van which they used to transport prisoners backwards and forwards from courts to prisons. Every time after that day whenever I saw a black mariah van on the road I used to look at the van, at the bars at the back and think of Mick sitting in it on his way to court. I was starting to feel really sick with worry by now . We were shown to a waiting room and I thought Oh no, I'm going to be sick. I rushed from the waiting room and just made it in time to the toilets. Even though I had been sick and years passed I often felt that same horrid sickly feeling about Mick and especially if I go anywhere near the court in Chester still today.

Don't know why I'm writing this now but Mick once said to me "Best not to eat a whole raw onion it will only end in tears!" Oh never mind, my mind goes all over the place at times.

Back to the court, when we had to go into the courtroom the judge had a white wig on which in itself to me at the time seemed very scary. Then they brought Mick up into the stand from the cells. It was the same dock that a few years previously Myra Hindley and Ian Brady had been sentenced from. I couldn't understand why Mick was in the same dock, he hadn't killed or harmed anyone. This nightmare just goes on and on. The cells are the original dungeons, no heating so very cold, they still had the original shackles on the cold stone walls – nightmarish.

Mick had three co-defendants up with him. I didn't know any of them, had never seen them with Mick. Sentence was passed. Mick got seven years for armed robbery, seven years for something else, seven years for another crime, four years for something else, two years and another one year. All in all he got sentenced to 28 years to run concurrently. I couldn't take it in. It was horrendous. The three other men – who had planned the robbery – all got lesser sentences. One of the co-defendants snitched on Mick saying it was his gun. They were all out of prison in a couple of years but no, not Mick. There are no words to describe exactly how I felt after listening to the sentence passed on Mick. My heart sank to my feet. All I could think of was seven years, seven long years – a lifetime. How am I going to cope with bringing our son Michael up on my own. The poor boy won't have his dad around anymore. No more rides on his dad's broad shoulders up to the newsagents on a weekend to get his sweets. I literally felt our lives had ended. That feeling has never really gone away after all these years. I still can't go anywhere near Chester Crown Court without feeling anxious. That day I ran out of the court in complete shock and terror. I couldn't understand how people outside were laughing and smiling, getting on and off buses, shopping etc. when my life had just ended the world was carrying on as normal. I remember seeing a lovely dress in the window of a boutique and thinking that if I bought it Mick would never see me in it. I felt desolate . When I got off the bus home in Little Sutton the newsagent where the robbery had taken place had a big billboard outside on the pavement with giant letters saying LOCAL MAN GETS 7 YEARS FOR ROBBERY. This was the final straw for me – my life as I knew it was over. I am not strong enough to carry on with this life. I couldn't even imagine doing the everyday basic things you take for granted like preparing meals, doing the shopping. It was a horrible, horrible time but I did find the strength to carry on and bring up Mike. I did survive. Ironically the hit song at the time was The Three Degrees – when will I see you again! Yes that was the question, when would I see him again?!

I want Mick, I want Mick. Those words went round and round in my head. For the next few days I was still in deep shock. I couldn't eat at all. I remember my mum cooked me bacon and tomatoes for my breakfast and I couldn't touch it. That was the morning of the day that my sister was taking me to the social services offices to explain my circumstances to them and see if I was eligible for any financial help. I remember someone in the waiting room was reading a newspaper with Mick's face splashed across the front of it, staring right out at me. It was a terrible nightmare I was in. Some assistance was available but in those days you didn't get your rent paid for you – you had to manage on the meagre amount they doled out to you.

After struggling for a couple of months and unable to continue paying the rent, Mike and I went back to live with mum and dad. I remember it was just before Xmas. Every few days I used to take Mike back to our old house and check on everything and see if there was any post but I could never stay there again without Mick. On one such visit I had just opened my front door when the lady next door came out to talk to me. She was about my age and had a little girl Mike's age. She told me her husband had seen someone trying to break into the house but had run away when he realised someone had seen him. She suggested I leave my front door key with her so they could check if anything was missing if a similar thing happened again. I readily agreed to this and arranged a hiding place for the key. A couple of months later when Mike and I went to check on our house I noticed the house next door looked empty. There were no curtains at the windows and everything appeared to have been moved out. In those days we called it a 'moonlight flit' when people were in debt they would just pack everything up in the middle of the night and disappear. I was a bit shocked but relieved when I found my front door key safe in its hiding place so I could still get in to my house. Straight away I noticed a couple of my beautiful glass vases had gone. Then I went into the kitchen and saw the toaster was missing together with a lovely red enamel jug with white hearts on it. My carpet sweeper had disappeared too and also some of my favourite LPs. I never told Mick or mum and dad about this but talk about hitting somebody when they are down – how could she have done this to us?

It was getting near to Xmas now and the number 1 song out was by Mud – it'll be lonely this Christmas without you by my side. I remember crying my eyes out and holding little Mike close to me whenever I heard it playing.

Mick used to write to us once a week – I used to call these letters good letter, bad letter. I suppose it all depended on Mick's mood at the time of writing and what had happened In prison around him – only natural I suppose. Eventually I got really anxious before I opened a letter – would it be good or bad? A good letter would be Mick telling me how much he loved me and Mike. A bad letter was Mick writing to tell me that he's lost some of his remission for bad behaviour. There were many, many times over the following years that Mick had to go to the Visiting Court where he lost more and more remission. Mick's old saying about eating a whole onion comes into my mind again and my God I ate a lot of Mick's raw onions in the years ahead and cried a lot of tears.

I ultimately lost our council house as the arrears gradually built up. It was such a struggle finding the money to pay the rent every week, plus the furniture HP debt and also Mick had a couple of suits waiting for him to pick up and pay for. Mick was also buying a car on finance from a man who lived at the top of our road and once he found out that Mick was in prison he came knocking on the door every time a payment was due and so I struggled on trying to make these debt payments. I didn't like that man at all. All in all money was very tight. I seem to remember the prison gave you a couple of pounds to enable you to pay for transport for visits to and from prison. It wasn't much though. Times were very hard for little Mike and I then.

The next time I saw Mick was in Hull prison in 1975. Mick's mum and dad took Mike and I on the train to see him. One of my memories of that day was a long train journey to a horrible dark grey old prison at the end of it. When we arrived in Hull we went out for some lunch and Mick's parents bought Mike some new clothes to wear to go and see his dad. I was looking forward to seeing Mick again but at the same time I had this horrible, horrible feeling of dread inside me, my stomach was in knots again. By this time Mick had already lost some of his remission due to his behaviour. We were sat in the waiting room looking forward to seeing Mick but when he came in his face was covered in bruises. I was so upset seeing him like that. He tried to laugh it off – telling me he had accidently walked into a door or something. At one point during the visit I remember saying to Mick if you keep on losing your remission and fighting you're never going to come out, you'll end up in a madhouse. How true were those words because three years later Mick was admitted to Broadmoor – a prison for the criminally insane. During the same visit another prisoner came over to us with some sweets and pop he had bought from the canteen for Mike. Afterwards Mick told me that the man was Charlie Wilson, one of the great train robbers, also doing time in Hull. After the visit ended I was once again inconsolable and little Mike was running after his dad again calling after Mick Daddy, daddy come back! It was heart-breaking. How the hell am I going to survive seven years of this I thought. It's said that when people are in prison and everything is taken away from them, they are told when to eat, when to sleep etc. their lives are hell trying to get used to their loss of liberties that everyone else takes for granted. In my experience it's a hell of a lot harder to be left on your own with a small child struggling to make a life for you both. I knew I could never ever experience anything like this again.

During those first few years when Mike and I were spending our time between my parent's house and our house in Little Sutton I often used to take Mike to Neston to see my brother's wife Pam. She had three small children and her mum, dear Mrs Jones, used to go there too to help Pam out with the children and give them their lunch. They already had a houseful but they made me and Mike so welcome. Everyday Mrs Jones made us lunch and fussed over us. Most of the time I was still very upset over Mick and she was always there with her hugs and to wipe my tears away. I'll never forget her, she tried to help me sort out my life as well as look after everyone else. She was a very special lady indeed – God bless her.

As the weeks turned into months and the months into years and Mick was still locked up, he continued sending me letters – the same good letters and bad letters whilst still losing his remission left, right and centre. In one of his letters he told me he'd been digging. I assumed he meant digging a pond somewhere within the prison grounds. He said as he was digging another prisoner came up behind him and stabbed him in the back. I'm not sure if this was in Broadmoor but anyway Mick couldn't just stand there and let him continue to stab him so he defended himself and overpowered the prisoner and took the knife away. It was Mick, however, who had to go to the Visiting Court even though he was acting in self defence. What else could I do he asked? This resulted in Mick losing all of his remaining remission. What a blow that was! When is he going to come out I asked myself – what are Mike and I going to do without him?

To try and cheer me up one day, my sister and her husband, Jan and Mike, who had just built a big bungalow on the outskirts of Helsby invited me to go and stay with them for a few days to take my mind off Mick. During the stay they were invited to a ball held by someone in the police force. Mike and Jan had been invited because Mike had been on the council and had a lot of ties with very well known people. They took me with them in the hope maybe that I would meet a nice, respectable policeman! I got all dolled up and wore a long scarf tied around my forehead which was a trendy thing to do at the time.

I certainly got a lot of attention but didn't meet anyone I wanted to get together with – I was still in love with Mick. How ironic that I should go to the police ball when my husband was in prison, obviously no-one knew that at the party! Golly, golly, golly!

Not long afterwards, Mick wrote to me and said that he had got into trouble again and had actually been given more time to do. He was very, very apologetic and kept on saying he'd had to defend himself when someone had confronted him with a piece of glass in his hand. Why oh why was it Mick who got more time on his sentence? That's prison for you – you either defend yourself from being attacked and you get punished by the authorities or do nothing and your life is made hell by the prison bullies. You'll be attacked more, raped, they'll dress you as a woman and gang rape you, all the horrors in the world will be unleashed on you. Mick said what else could he do, what choice did he have either protect and defend yourself or give in to abuse – you can't win either way. What a choice to have to make. In the letter Mick said it would be best if I divorced him! He said he was never going to get out ; he loved me and Mike so much but it wasn't a good life for us struggling with money waiting for him to come out of prison - which may never happen as has been proved 45 years later and he's still there. If he had murdered people or was a terrorist he would have been let out years ago. It just doesn't seem fair.

Eventually I agreed with Mick, it would be best to divorce him as it seemed unlikely he would ever be coming out. I didn't do anything about the divorce for a couple of years though. I just kept going through the Yellow Pages looking for divorce lawyers. I would make an appointment then chicken out and not go ahead with it. This happened so many times but finally I did keep an appointment and eventually divorced him but it was a long time after Mick had suggested it.

In the meantime I was starting to wish that I hadn't lost touch with all my old school friends which had happened after I married Mick. I used to see women my age going out and about in the evenings and I always wished I had someone to go for a night out with. Then I had a brill idea! Mum and Dad used to get the |Liverpool Echo and I noticed all these adverts in it such as man looking for woman for romance, woman looking for woman for friendship to go out with etc. So I got in touch with this woman called Trisha. She was new to the area and was looking for someone to go out with for evenings out too so we arranged to meet up and straightaway we hit it off. She was the area sales manager for Cousins (beauty products not the cafes) and was very pretty and had a lovely little car. We had a flipping ball of a time we really did!

Just before I answered her advert in the Echo I thought it would be a great idea to get a job as a barmaid. I'd never done anything like it before but I thought it was a way of getting out of the house and meeting people. I saw an advert in a local paper asking for a barmaid at Westwood Grange in Thornton Hough not far from mum and dads house in little Neston. Westwood Grange was a large country house used as a country club with a nightclub downstairs with a large bar and a bar upstairs set in an open lounge area near the entrance doors. It had a lovely old fashioned spiral staircase and on the landing area sat a large parrot which used to talk to everyone who went past on their way to the toilets! It was a great place and in the years to come I would have many, many great nights out there. I walked in through these big entrance doors and the manager walked up to meet me. I told him I had an interview - he just looked at me and said you can start on Saturday night! I was made up! It was the easiest interview I had ever had, no difficult questions only how soon could I start!

Saturday arrived and I started my new job at the big bar by the entrance doors. It was also really busy – jam-packed in fact – it was one of those trendy places, along with Leighton Court, where people went to be seen. I'm afraid me and bar work did not go together at all! I could never get the sharp bottle caps off the bottles with the opener on the bar. I usually ended up breaking the glass bottle in my attempts and as for remembering what everyone had ordered I continually got the orders mixed up; oh no, I definitely didn't like bar work at all! I used to get so flustered that whenever a customer told me to keep the change or have a drink myself, I rang all the money up in the till including my tips. I didn't like the work at all even though I did meet a lot of men and went on some dates with them during my time there.
When I met Trisha I handed my notice in at Westwood Grange but returned many times there as a customer with her.

During this time Mick's letters and my replies started to dwindle away. Mick's mum and dad continued to pick Mike up and take him out for the day. I was never around to see them when they came back. I felt as though they were very disappointed in me for divorcing Mick , even though they often used to say to me over the years that if Mick couldn't prove himself in jail I would be better off divorcing him.

Things carried on in this way for several more years; in the meantime I was having a ball with Trisha. She appeared very money motivated – she seemed to have the knack of smelling out money. She seemed to have an inbuilt radar to find rich men and knew which clubs to go to in Manchester, Liverpool and Chester. She also received a lot of invitations to go to gigs and events as a VIP. It was amazing and certainly opened my eyes!
I remember one night she picked me up and we went to a club in Manchester called Blinkers. It wasn't long before these two men were buying us champagne. One of them was mixed race and very handsome and his friend was smaller but with a lovely head of thick black hair. I wasn't really into the smaller man but I went out with him a couple of times as a foursome with Trisha and the other guy. They both had dead posh new cars and took us to lovely restaurants and clubs. Trisha's bloke actually had his own plane! She'd certainly sniffed out the money with this one! I was just friends with the other man, no romantic

interest there but just seeing him so that Trisha could meet up with her bloke. Anyway, one night my bloke picked me up in his posh sports car and then pulled in for fuel at the garage on the Chester High Road. He got out of the car and started to walk towards the petrol pump when suddenly there was a gust of wind and the next thing was omg this man was completely bald! Unbeknown to me he wore a wig and the wind had dislodged it! Oh no, his hair had been the most attractive thing about him I just stayed with him that night when we met up with the other two. They took us to a club in Liverpool called Uglys. From the outside it didn't look like a club it just looked like a terraced house with an ordinary front door Where on earth are we going I wondered. Apparently you had to be invited or already a member to go inside, but once inside it was amazing with a great big long dance floor and bars but after that night I couldn't bring myself to make up a foursome again. I couldn't rid myself of the sight of his wig blowing off in the wind!

On another night out in Manchester with Trisha we went to this place with a big circular bar in the middle with tables all around it. We were both standing at the bar when a bloke standing at the bar kept staring and smiling at me. He was quite nice looking with longish dark hair but I thought he was too small. I prefer taller men so I just wasn't interested in him at all and suggested to Trisha we go somewhere else. So we left and went to this other place then Trisha told me that the bloke who had been smiling at me was in fact George Best and he owned the bar we had just been in.!

We were certainly having a great social life! We had so many dates with so many men we used to wish there were more days in the week to fit them all in. At one point I was going out with three different men – Chester Dave, nice car Dave and Dave who I eventually married. We sometimes went to a fab country house outside Manchester in lovely grounds. We used to go on a Saturday and check in and book a room so we could stay over night. Saturday night was a big club night. To get to the nightclub part you had to walk along corridors which looked like white caves. It had different bars including a champagne bar we used to have a ball there. After we checked in we would have a glass of wine we had brought with us and play some music while we got ready for our big night out. At one time my friend and I were dating two members of the Red Arrows . This particular night they were doing a big air display in Manchester on the Sunday and we both watched them going through their check list outside our windows. Mine liked to call me Pocahontas because the night I met him I had a gold band tied around my forehead. Bredbury Hall it was called, I've just remembered it now! Oh what fun we all had on our nights out. At other times we met celebrities from soaps and I made a lot of really good friends. When we used to go out in Chester we met up in a bar by the canal and from there we used to walk to a big gay nightclub called Alchemy and amazing times were had by all.

I know this sounds too good to be true but it was truly amazing. It was

a time for me that helped me to let go of my past and try and forget all about Mick. I just had to block that part of my life out in order for me to heal.
During this time Mick appeared in the news a few times but I had to block Mick out of my head as difficult as that was.

When I met Dave who I later married I thought here we go, I had better go to a solicitor and get my divorce started now Mick and I are over I've got to move on for myself and little Michael. I plucked the courage up to get a solicitor and I got a court date at Birkenhead Court for my divorce. This day all the cases were for uncontested divorces and just one person appeared for each divorce. Because my name was Peterson I was one of the last cases to be heard. I sat there terrified listening to the judge who I thought was really stern and quite nasty to people before me on the list. He was making snidey remarks to everyone and I though OMG how nasty he is, what on earth is he going to say to me about our case?

My turn eventually came. I had to stand up in front of the judge and read my solicitors remarks about the reason for wanting a divorce. Then he said "Oh no, the poor man, oh no he's in Walton, oh dear no, that's not the most salubrious of her Majesty's hotels! Poor chappie. What the hell, I thought?! Even my solicitor mentioned it to me afterwards. I don't know why the judge made those remarks but, hey, never mind, it's all over now.

Soon after this I made the decision (and I must say much to my detriment and Michael's) to stop all contact with Mick and Mick's mum and dad and family. I really thought I was doing the right thing at the time because I was worried Mick's parents would take Mike to see him in jail or talk about Mick to him and traumatise him. I really thought Mike would get frightened and confused if he continued to see them. With the benefit of hindsight I realise I made one of the biggest mistakes of my life. I even sent Mick a form to sign from my solicitor to stop any contact between them. Mick signed it without reading it, thinking it was just another divorce form that required his signature. Apparently, when Mick first received the divorce forms and my accompanying letter, the prison warder threw them at him in his cell and said to him "even your wife doesn't want you now". Ah poor Mick, one blow after another for him, how cruel was I! I stopped Mick's parents from seeing their only grandson and just after they had lost a son to the prison service. I often think how devastated I would be if anyone stopped me from seeing either of my grandchildren. God forgive me.

Thinking back over this today I know Mike suffered so much from the loss of his other family but I found out later that my mum and dad used to speak on the phone to Mick's parents from time to time and sent them photos of Mike as he was growing up. I will always regret my decision to stop and between them and know now how very wrong it is to do so. I always tell people with children who split up to let both parents and grandparents see them. It's no good saying, "Oh he doesn't deserve to see them, he didn't do this, he didn't do that!" but a child should always see both its parents and extended family, even if its only now and again – a child does need that contact. My thoughts at the time were that now I was going to get married to Dave and Michael was going to have a new dad and little sister (I was pregnant at the time) that the past didn't matter any more and we should concentrate on our new life and be like a normal family. How innocent and ignorant I was, how very wrong I was, we would never be able to forget about Mick! I don't think that even one day passed in the coming years that I didn't think about Mick or something would remind me of him.

Chapter Seven: My New Family

I met Dave my second husband at Westwood Grange, he was a local lad but had just come back home after years travelling around in Australia. It was Christmas Eve and I had gone there with a few friends for a night out. We dated for a while and then arranged to get married at Birkenhead Registry Office. I bought my dress – a long cream maxi dress – from Birkenhead market. I also saw a lovely matching cream handbag the same colour as the dress which I really wanted but couldn't afford at the time so I went and did a very stupid thing. I found a pawn shop nearby and pawned my lovely white gold patterned wedding ring Mick had bought me for £3. £3 - what was I like! The exact price of the handbag I wanted! And even worse, I didn't even think about going to get it back later. Something I've always regretted.

When we fixed the date to get married I had expected my Decree Absolute to have come through but oh no, the date came for my final decree and I never received it. I rang the registry office and said I still hadn't received my Decree Absolute and the man on the phone went mad with me telling me I wasn't supposed to arrange another marriage until that decree is in my hands! He said he was fed up with people ringing him up for their decrees so they could remarry but at that time there was some sort of postal strike on and this delayed some of the paperwork. I was frantic at this delay. There I was pregnant and unable to get married on the day we had arranged. Ah but you know what, my dad was so good to me, he saw I was frantic so he rang Dave up with some excuse about having to rearrange the date of the wedding and the ceremony took place a little while later. Ah, love you dad, you really made up for your temper over the years, you came good for me! God bless him. We had the reception at mum and dad's house. A picture appeared in Cheshire Life of us – Irene, youngest daughter of Mr and Mrs Kelsey of Sandy Lane, Little Neston! A very different occasion than my first marriage.

Mike and Dave never really got on right from the start. Mike used to tell Dave to get away from his mummy if he tried to sit down by me or cuddle me. As the years passed I overheard Dave telling Mike that he was sorry for not trying harder to get on with him but he explained it by saying it was the same as a lion having cubs but Mike wasn't his real cub. It didn't sound as harsh as that and in a way it was a nice apology to Mike but I was always on edge when the two of them were together. It's very hard when you have a step-parent; hard for the child, for the step parent and especially for the mother. You feel that the father is being harder on your child than his own children. It's a difficult thing to come to terms with.

Around about this time my OCD started to get a lot worse. As well as touching objects over and over again in a repetitive pattern, I started to stand up and sit down over and over again, sometimes as much as twenty times at a time. If anyone was in the room they would wonder what I was doing but anyone who has OCD will know it's a difficult thing to explain because the condition means you have to wait a bit and then do it all over again, it's a compulsion. Funnily enough when I met another partner much later on I just stopped doing it and have never done the standing up and sitting down thing again!

After Dave and I were married Mike never mentioned his dad again. I think he didn't want to upset me and I didn't mention Mick to him either for the same reason. Was I right in doing so, or was I wrong? I totally did think I was doing the right thing at the time but looking back again with the benefit of hindsight I realise how wrong I was. I've made so many mistakes over the years but please realise these were not normal circumstances – this is Mick we're talking about! I found out much later on that someone had told Mike his dad was a big bright star in the sky shining down on him. Mike actually mentions this in a magazine article he did a while back but I knew nothing about this at the time.

When Michael was about eight years old, he went to the sweet shop round the corner with Dave's dad. I was at home watching the news on the television when a piece about Broadmoor came and and I swear to God that it showed Mick walking along a corridor. It was shot from the back and you couldn't see his face but I recognised his walk and his voice. I was in shock, I was shaking and so upset it had unsettled me but I was so relieved that Mike hadn't seen it.

Whatever I was doing it never left me, always there at the back of my mind. I used to have terrible nightmares about myself escaping from prison and climbing all those high walls with gangsters running after me. I would wake up hot and sweaty and terrified. I used to wake up in the night and go into the kitchen to get a cup of tea to calm myself down. If Dave, or my future partner, came in to see if I was alright, I would call them Mick. I did that so many times I didn't know who I was married to when I woke up. Mick was always on my mind one way or another.

It also didn't help that Mike looked exactly like his dad. He had his dad's colouring, his lovely brown eyes, even some of Mick's expressions so that whenever I looked at Mike I saw Mick. If I opened a newspaper or turned on the television there was Mick. He was everywhere. There didn't seem to be anywhere I could go without being reminded of Mick. This went on for all the coming years; in fact it's still going on now – 46 years later! Was I still in love with Mick then, I'll never know but it hurt deep down in my soul. I'd be worrying about Mike and worrying about Mick wasting his whole life away in prison for just a few petty crimes. I was always brought back to the past, it was so hard to move on and look towards a better future under those circumstances.

I was living in Heswall now with my new family but whenever I went back to my parent's house I used to read the newspapers as they had them delivered daily. I could never believe it but every time I picked up a paper there was always a page or pages missing. When I asked mum and dad about the missing pages dad always blamed it on the incompetent paper boy! He would say he's useless that lad he manages to lose half the paper before he delivers it! I believed this to be true for many, many years until Mike was a lot older and then guess what! I found myself doing the exact same thing mum and dad used to do – taking out any pages in the paper with stories about Mick in them. They were doing it to protect me as I was trying to protect Mike . Ah, bless them.

Another day I'd taken Mike to visit mum and dad. Mike had gone off fishing with some of his friends and we'd just finished eating our lunch and dad had the lunchtime news on the television. The next minute I saw on the tv Mick on top of the roof at Broadmoor hospital! It was too late for dad to switch it off so he passed it off as though it didn't matter and tried to get me to smile but I couldn't. My heart had dropped to my feet. Oh Mick, I just wished he would hurry up and get out of there. I was so upset but also relieved that Mike hadn't seen his dad up there. Obviously Mick's former job as an industrial painter was ideal practice for climbing. He had to climb massive pylons and large industrial petroleum tanks to paint them. Climbing the roof at Broadmoor to make a roof-top protest at his treatment there was easy for him. Mick has climbed more roofs than Santa Claus! He climbed the roof at Parkhurst once, Broadmoor twice , Wandsworth, Hull, Walton and Winchester. In fact, I think he climbed the roof at Wandsworth three times in total and also Leicester prison roof. He could climb like a monkey, there's no doubt about that at all.

Years went by with no contact from Mick at all. There were still loads of stories about Mick in all the papers though. Some were frightening saying he was another Hannibal Lecter, he eats people, constantly kicking off , taking people hostage etc. He did in fact take three Iraqi prisoners hostage. They had hijacked a plane full of people and children and been sentenced and sent to whichever prison Mick was in at the time. Mick took them hostage and guess what – Mick had another seven years added to his sentence for taking the hijackers hostage and the hijackers themselves were sentenced to three years when their hostages were a whole plane full of innocent people. Where's the justice in that, hey? I was so worried about the type of man prison had changed Mick into. I was silly enough at that time to believe all the stories I read in the newspapers. I kept trying to block out my past with Mick but I couldn't, it came coming back to haunt me again and again.

One day Mike and I were at home watching television when a woman called Saira was being interviewed. She had her young daughter with her and was talking about how she and Mick planned to get married. This was a big shock to me and also to Mike as it seemed to come out of the blue but we had no contact with Mick and so he had no reason to tell us. What really upset me and especially Mike was that she said on camera that Mick had always wanted children and that now he would have her daughter. I was furious, how cruel was she to say that, completely ignoring the fact that Mick had a son – Mike, his own flesh and blood. I just don't know how a woman, and a mother at that, could cruelly act as though her new partner's son didn't exist. I was upset but poor Mike was devastated. I thought Mike had gone through hell over the years because of his dad and now here was this woman acting as though her daughter was the only child Mick had and Mike didn't exist. I'm damn sure that she knew all about Mike and couldn't understand why she would be so cruel.

I can remember at the time I'd just be watching one of the soaps on tv and I'd once more get the urge to stand up and sit down repeatedly again – obviously brought on by the stress of all this. My son JD was only talking about this the other day and we both thought that extreme behaviour was probably brought on originally by all the anxiety and worry about Mick and Mike.

Just to bring you back to the present day, I jumped on a bus this morning to drop some flowers and a book called Jesus Calling off to an old family friend, dear Christine. I just knocked on her door then left them on her step. I hopped back on a bus to Heswall and had this strong urge to have fish and chips for my lunch! It was only just opening time and I didn't want to go in too early – in case they gave me all the old chips from the day before! So I had a browse around the Valentine cards at Tesco. Why Valentine cards I had no idea – I had no-one to buy one for but I looked anyway to pass some time before going back to the chippy for my fish and chips – mmmmm yummy! They were lovely too, nice and fresh and I really enjoyed them. ANYWAY, the point of this story is that when I gave my name in with my food order the Greek man serving me said Oh Irene – did you know that you have a Greek name? He then pronounced it the Greek way – don't ask me to pronounce it I have trouble with a lot of English words! – but he said it means PEACE. Oh how lovely is that! I was made up with it, but now going back over the years I think 'peace' was always the last thing on my mind or in my life. Oh well, never mind. How lovely! PEACE, PEACE TO ALL.

Chapter Eight: Spirits

Whilst I was married to Dave I had two more children, James and Leicia. They both got on really well with Mike and looked up to him as their older brother. They are still very close to this day. Whenever I took Leicia out in her pram Mike used to stand guard over her. He used to say to people "You get away from my sister", he was very protective. In those days you couldn't take prams into shops because they were a lot bigger than they are nowadays – but it was a lot safer than it is today.

As the three kids grew up we became aware that there were spirits in the house we were living in. We all saw at different times, an old woman, an old man and a little boy who appeared to always be on his knees praying (or so we thought at the time). May times I tried to find out who these people were. It transpired the old man and woman used to live in the house but I could never trace who the little boy was. There was never a record of a little boy having lived in the house in the past.

I used to suffer when I was younger with very bad coughs. If I went near anyone with a cold you could guarantee I would end up with my bad cough. At these times when I had a bad cough, Dave always moaned about it in bed at night, so I felt much more comfortable making a bed on the settee in the lounge in order to cough in peace! Quite often on these occasions I used to have horrible, frightening experiences. I used to feel someone lying on top of me and on one time I remember this spirit lying on top of me and trying to kiss me on my mouth. I was absolutely terrified, its breath smelled like he had been dead for years – which he actually had been! I got up and just ran back to my bedroom anything was better than staying in the lounge with the spirit – I would just have to annoy Dave with my coughing. Ug, I can still remember how vile its breath smelt, the spirit that is not Dave. Nightmarish.

There was still no direct contact with Mick in those days but the papers were full of all sorts of stories about Mick, some of which were very worrying and frightening for Mike and I. We couldn't separate the truth from the fiction and we were both scared.

Dave and Mike were still not getting on too well, another big constant worry for me. Many times if they were both in the house together I would stand outside the door of whichever room they were in and listen, just in case they were arguing. I couldn't rest until I knew they were getting on alright. It was hard.

Another time Mike and Dave had fallen out big time and Dave had banned Mike from the house. This particular day Dave had gone out to work and Mike had popped round to see me. The next thing is Dave had forgotten something and came back home then stayed for a couple of hours. As soon as we heard Dave's car pulling up outside the house Mike went and hid from Dave in the garage. I remember being terrified that Dave would go into the garage for something and find Mike here. I seemed to be living on my nerves all the time.

I heard a ghost fart but it never smelt: Charlie Salvador

46

It was a horrible time for both Mike and myself. It was always on my mind that Dave wasn't Mike's real dad and that situation is hard to deal with. Looking back now there were some good times when Mike was a lot younger. Mike was a very keen fisherman, he knew everything there was to know about fishing, he still loves it now. My dad had his own fishing boat years before so maybe he took after him. When Mike was about ten or eleven years old he joined a fishing club and they used to have fishing matches in Birkenhead Park. Dave and Dave's dad used to take him there every week and very often Mike would win a competition. It seemed that as Mike grew older the clashes with Dave grew worse.

When the kids were older I started a part-time job at Ethel Austin in Heswall, a clothing retailer. Three cheers for Ethel Austins! I always used to buy my mum's big knickers and support tights from there and, of course, it was great for kids' clothes and underwear. The girls who worked there were lovely, we had many great times together at work or when we used to go out to the Johnny Pye after work for a drink or two. We always seem to get a lot of regular customers who became friends of ours. There was one couple who really stood out – a mother and daughter who used to come in regularly to see if we had any new bargains in the shop. To be honest, they were a bit strange looking. They both had short, jet black hair but they both were so lovely. One day a lady came into work and asked me if she could take a photograph of me, there and then in my Ethel Austin's uniform and my hair in plaits. She was taking photos of people who were well known in Heswall. I was well known for riding my bike everywhere and for having my long black hair in plaits. She also took photos of the mother and daughter that used to come into the shop. She was going to paint large oil paintings from all the photos she'd taken and then put them up on the wall of a little café nearby that had just opened. Obviously, I couldn't wait to see the painting so I went in to the café with mum and the kids and there staring right at me, was me in all my glory! Mum asked the lady who had painted it if she could buy it. The woman said yes but it would cost about £300 and in those days that was an awful lot of money. Sadly, we couldn't afford to buy it but we did think what use would the painting of me be when she took it off the wall. Such a shame.

One of our regular customers, a man we used to call the knicker feeler, used to come into the shop and feel the ladies' thongs that were hanging up on a rail. He would walk past them touching the crotch of every pair, eeeh it was sick. The odd thing was though on each of these visits he would buy a small pair of thongs but the strange thing was his wife was enormous and no way could wear them. Weird hey, what the hell was he up to with that small thong. Oh well, never mind hey.

During this time the spirits in my house only showed themselves about once every three months but on Easter Sunday I was in work and I needed to go upstairs to the stockroom to get something. This room used to be where the projectionist used to play the films to people in the cinema. Nothing had changed there since the cinema closed down many years before. I forgot to mention that before the shop was Ethel Austins it was a cinema and then Lennons. Anyway, I said to the girls in a jokey way I'm just popping up to the stock room – if I'm not back in an hour the ghost has got me! How psychic was I! I didn't even know there was actually a spirit up there, the spirit of an old projectionist it was. Don't ask me how I knew but I do know I could even draw a picture of him: a little bent over old man even though I never saw him. Anyway, there I was on my knees looking through a box of black leggings for a customer as we didn't have her size on the shop floor. The next thing I felt dead weird, I knew someone was by me even though no-one had gone through the alarmed door. Then I saw a black blur just move past me, that's the only way I can describe it, and I was so cold I was shaking. My eyes were running badly and I felt as though I was sitting in a freezer. Oh my God, I knew I had to run down those stairs really quickly and I was terrified. It was not a nice experience at all. I ran down those stairs and the manageress came running up to me. Oh Irene she said, you look as though you've just seen a ghost! I have I said, it's an old man upstairs in the stockroom. She could see I was really frightened and she took me into our little office. As she leant over to put the kettle on to make me a cup of tea I started to feel really, really cold again and I couldn't stop shaking I was so cold. I started crying my eyes out again because of the cold. "Sarah, Sarah" I shouted he's here, he's standing right by you. She took me into her private office and locked the door (not that a lock would have stopped him. I'm telling you now she definitely felt the spirit too and was getting frightened like me. For weeks after that she would never switch all the lights off when she closed the shop, she was too scared to come in on her own in the dark too. Sarah's mum gave her something (I can't remember what it was) but she had to leave it at the bottom of the stairs – it was supposed to stop the spirit from going up the stairs to our little room and office.

I found out months later that I was right, we did have a spirit of an old man in our stock room, when the shop was Lennons a couple of the girls who worked there said they had also seen the little old man quite often in the stockroom, but he was friendly. No, I definitely did not get the feelings of friendship - I was terrified. Not long after this I saw an advert in a women's magazine asking if anyone had any ghost stories they wanted to share. I wrote my ghost story down and sent it to them and they published it under the title 'Don't go into the Stockroom'! Ehhhh

On a lighter note, when I was working at Ethel Austin the girls there planned a surprise to celebrate my 50th birthday. They made me go home from work early in the afternoon so I couldn't see what they were up to and arranged to pick me up later on around 4.30 in the afternoon to take me back to work. What was this all about? Anyway, my manager picked me up at the agreed time and took me back to work. Before we got out of her car she insisted on tying a blindfold over my eyes. I had to leave it on until she led me into the shop and then they took my blindfold off. I couldn't believe my eyes! They had cleared the shop floor and made a party aisle for me with balloons and streamers everywhere! Right at the bottom of the party aisle was a table set with all sorts of lovely party food. I was so taken aback but the best surprise was still to come! There was a lovely bike decorated in balloons for me. God, I was so touched, and so happy as I desperately needed another bike as the chain was always coming off my old one. So there was I, on my birthday, riding my new bike up and down a party aisle at Ethel Austins! It is a very precious and treasured memory for me and always will be. Ah, how lovely of them all, bless them.

About a week after my birthday they had also planned a day out in Blackpool for me. They had hired a minivan to take us there and back and what a great time we all had. We did everything that you could do in Blackpool. We went to the fair, a restaurant and pub, a long walk on the prom and the beach and a browse around the shops. The day was jam packed with fun and laughter. We had fish and chips for our lunch, it was amazing. The girls all wanted me to go on the fairground horses. Yes I can do that I thought it's what the little kids go on so I got on this horse with the other girls but I made a BIG MISTAKE: I chose a horse on the outside which meant it went a lot faster than ones on the inside. Oh my God, I was so scared !I kept screaming 'Make it stop! Make it stop!' but the more I screamed the faster the operator made it go. Everyone, including my work mates were in hysterics. They couldn't stop laughing at me but I'll tell you this I was so glad when the ride stopped. Oh well, never mind hey! What beautiful memories they made for me. They also made a photo album with all the pictures of Blackpool in, how fab was that! Ah, how I miss those girls.

Another time when I was working at Ethels, one of my aunties phoned me up to say that a man had phoned them asking if they were any relation to me and if so could they give him my phone number. Of course they didn't do that and asked him to give them his phone number for me to contact if I wanted to. He said he was an old friend of Micks and he was trying to get in touch with me so that Mick could get in touch with his son Mike – this was after 26 years of no contact. Oh no, I thought, who the hell is this man? Is he a murderer, who is he? Is he a prisoner? I was terrified wondering who he was so in the end I plucked up the courage to ring him and find out what's going on. I was worried if I was doing the right thing but I eventually made the call and spoke to this man. His name was Ray Williams and he ended up becoming a very good friend to Mike and myself in later years. Sadly he died a few years ago and Mike and I went to his funeral. It was a lovely service, God bless him.

At the time I was scared for myself and for Mike. We'd had no contact with Mick for so long and all the information we had about him was what we read in the media – all those mad fantasy stories about this mad man who ate people. A crazy man. Shall I tell Mike, should I tell Mike? I didn't know what to do for the best. Eventually I decided I had to tell Mike that his dad wanted to get in touch with him again after all these years, 26 in all. I felt Mike had a right to know and he was old enough to make his own decisions. So we had a chat about it and Mike decided that, yes he did want to be in touch with his dad again. Ray arranged to go with Mike to visit Mick in prison. The meeting went well I think, thank God. If your wondering how the visit went for Mike, well that's Mike's story to tell, if he wants to tell it.

Today is February 15th. This is a big milestone for Mick; his request for parole is going to be heard in the Crown Court, London in a public parole hearing. I do so hope he is granted his request he soooo deserves it. All his other parole hearings have been heard behind closed doors with the decision already made. It's time he was out and gets it out to the public what really goes on inside Mick's prisons. Keep your fingers crossed for him! Good news! Mick has been allowed in Court to put his parole hearing before the public sometime later this year. It still has to go through the court again but it looks as though he's one step nearer to his freedom. Thank you God.

Chapter Nine: Anyone Want A Pea?

One day when I was at work in Ethels I received a phone call, it was from The Trisha Show – anyone remember The Trisha Show? It was before Jeremy Kyle. It was a phone call from one of their team asking me if I would appear on a programme they were filming called 'Bad Boys'. It wasn't the normal style of reality show where you had couples arguing amongst themselves, they just wanted me to talk about Mick. They offered me and a friend a stay overnight in a posh hotel with breakfast the following morning and so I agreed to do it. I had to be ready to be picked up from home the following day to travel down to London. That's the only thing about those sort of shows, they ask you to appear and when you agree they want to pick you up immediately which means you don't have much time to get yourself prepared or have your hair, nails done, etc. So to say I was in a panic was an understatement, I was in a really big panic. Anyway, after work that day I washed my hair and sorted out which clothes to wear so I was ready to be picked up by one of their taxis. I took my daughter Leicia with me and we had such a laugh on the long journeys to and from the studio.

It was that time of year, summer months and Tesco were selling bags of fresh garden peas, which I love! Most people would buy sweets, crisps, chocolate etc. to take on the journey but not me, I bought a couple of big bags of peas in their pods. You see, when Dad was alive we had such a big garden that Dad used to grow rows and rows of all types of vegetables including peas. I would go into the garden and work my way along the pea plants and fill my stomach to my heart's content. When dad died Mum sold the big house and bought a bungalow with a much smaller garden, so it was the end of the peas fresh from the garden for me. I always had to buy them from the supermarket instead. Many times on the journey to the studio and back, I was asking the driver does anyone want a nice pea!.

I can't remember at the moment where Trisha's studio was but it took us about three hours to get there. When we finally arrived at our posh hotel it was beautiful. It was quite late at night so Leicia and I just went to bed so I'd be nice and fresh in the morning for the interview. I awoke, put my makeup on and got myself ready for my appearance as we were getting picked up at 9am to go to the studio. On the journey on the way down the researchers were constantly asking me this and that about my life with Mick.

Anyway, we arrived at the studio and were put into a small lounge-like room. We were not allowed to leave this room without first asking permission from a team member. To be honest, I felt as though I was sort of locked up in this room, it was weird but obviously this was a regular part of the routine with guests on the Trisha Show because some of the guests may have got themselves drunk or just disappeared and as it was filmed live I suppose this was a necessary precaution to take. Then a lady came and took me to the makeup room. Now, bear in mind it was summer and I had a nice tan and I don't wear foundation, I thought oh no, what are they going to do with me! I explained I didn't normally wear foundation and the makeup lady said I had to wear it because of the studio lighting. I reluctantly gave in and let her put all this pink – yes pink! – foundation thickly all over my face. I remember saying to her this pink stuff looks terrible on my skin and she finally agreed that it didn't look right on me and started taking some of it off. I'm not kidding you I looked as if I was wearing a mask with holes cut out for my eyes. When my daughter saw me she said 'oh mum, what have they done to you.? They've hidden your tan too, you looked lovely this morning before you went into makeup.' This makeup experience has always stayed with me , especially in future years when I appeared again on TV but luckily I've always had lovely makeup artists doing my makeup the way I do it myself and no more mishaps. Thank God for that.

It was quite a wonderful experience on the Trisha Show beside the makeup mix-up. Trisha popped into the little guest lounge to have a chat before we went on air. Leicia sat with the studio audience and I went and sat with Trisha on the stage. At this point I'd like to say that I have never ever said anything horrible about Mick to any of the media. Trisha did try to get me to say otherwise but in vain. There was a man in the audience who said Mick was a wrong 'un and that I was too scared to say anything against him. That was his opinion, he obviously didn't know Mick and simply believed everything he had read about Mick in the press as do a lot of people. In fact, Trisha said to me on air before the interview ended that she thought that I was still in love with Mick. I had told Trisha beforehand that I had remarried but she still asked me that. Why ??? Am I ???

The taxi picked us up from the studio after the show and we had some sandwiches and refreshments with some of the other guests from the show. The taxi driver was so funny, the three of us were definitely on top form, making jokes, laughing our heads off , eating peas yummmm! That was my first experience of being filmed on TV but it wasn't to be my last.

About a year later Chanel 4 and Chanel 5 were ringing me asking if I would appear on a documentary they wanted to make about Mick. The offered to pay me for it and I think at the time they were both competing to get the most tv ratings. I remember one of them came on at about 11pm the night before the one I agreed to do so came on tv, the one before was very violent. Some footage had been sneaked out of Mick's prison and you could see quite a lot of his treatment there. It showed the heavy mob beating him up – about 15 to 20 of them at a time. It was very, very upsetting to see. When I went into Tesco the following day so many complete strangers came up to me to say how shocked they had been to see what really had been going on inside these prisons and the things that had happened to Mick. They said it had changed their opinion of him rather than reading so much fantasy news in the media. I actually refused to be in that violent documentary. I felt uncomfortable with not knowing if anything I said may be twisted out of context. I was actually in bed when the programme aired and Leicia came running into my bedroom saying mum you're on television and sure enough there were some photos of me when I was younger and still married to Mick. I did continue to watch it myself then too but I felt as though the documentary maker was annoyed because I had refused to appear on it. It started off by saying that 'Irene went to see Mick to tell him that their marriage was over' when in fact I didn't go and see Mick in prison, I wrote to him. They implied that Mick then went back into his cell and wrecked it. This was the beginning of Mick turning into Bronson and it implied that it was my fault although that wasn't actually stated. A lot of my friends said to me so it was your fault Mick turned into Bronson? Oh well, never mind hey!

On my documentary on Chanel 4 or 5, I say my documentary but members of Mick's family and Mike and I also appeared on it, it really got the point across, showing the truth about what was really going on inside the prisons where Mick was. It was a great documentary. I was filmed in Ellesmere Port by the river Mersey but I didn't recognise the area at all. It had all been done up and posh apartments were built there. The water was glistening in the sunshine giving me a lovely background. In fact the team who did the filming said it was one of the nicest interviews they had ever done. Before the filming though, Mike, Leicia and I had had a drink in a local pub with the crew. They were really lovely and put us at ease. They filmed Mike's interview in a hilly, grassy area with a train going past every now and then in the background and played fab music to match the scene but they had to stop the filming because this bloke who was nearby decided to do a streak! He threw all his clothes off and ran right in front of us. It was hilarious! I felt very comfortable doing this documentary because I didn't feel under any pressure and was allowed to say what I wanted to say. Of course, I had made my notes so they kept stopping the filming so I could read through my notes again. Yes, I was very pleased with it. I bought a nice dress to wear – I can't remember the name of the boutique – and I bought matching clip-on earrings and everyone said how lovely I looked. At a later time I went back to the same boutique looking for another dress and the assistant said they had had a few women coming into the shop trying to buy the same dress because I had worn it on television. That's a nice compliment, isn't it!

Before these documentaries were shown on tv I was at work at Ethels one day. I was on the till that day which was positioned right by the front door so anyone entering the shop would have to walk past me. I had my hair in my usual Ethel Austin style of two long plaits. Then the buzzer at the till went off, it was our staff buzzer. The manageress was calling me and said 'Irene, take your name badge off now and come up to the office straightaway'. Oh my God, I thought, what have I done now? And why do I have to take my name badge off? When I went up to the office, the manageress told me that the press were here and wanted to know if I was in work. She then told me to put my coat on and quickly sneak out at the door at the rear of the shop so no-one would see me and follow me. That was an experience I'd never had before. When I arrived home there was a letter from the Mirror newspaper waiting for me. I opened it and found they wanted to do a story on me and were offering a large sum of money for me to spill the beans on my life with Mick. They said it would be better for me to cooperate with them rather than the other newspapers. The odd thing was they had walked right past me when they first came into the shop whilst I was still wearing my name badge! I never took them up on their offer at that time, I didn't want to upset my mum or Mike or any other family member.

There was an incident when Mike was a lot older, again I can't go into details as it's Mike's story to tell if he decides to tell it, but it did affect me mentally very badly. I just had the urge to scream my head off. The urge was overwhelming and I would go into my bedroom and just scream and scream. A little voice inside my head kept urging me on. 'Go on scream, scream' it said and between the screams I was swearing my head off. I felt as though I was possessed or something, it was really bad but I knew at one point that if I didn't stop doing it I would go right over the edge and have a complete breakdown. Somehow, I found the strength from somewhere to stop this behaviour. I survived. I'm a survivor but I remember for quite a few weeks after that there was always a member of my family with me wherever I went or whatever I did just in case it happened again. They were so worried about me.

Many years later I saw an advert on TV for Big Brother auditions and thought to myself 'why not, I'm going to audition for it' . I arrived at the venue in Manchester on a Saturday morning but my heart dropped when I saw a line of people queuing up for miles outside the audition building. Oh my God, so many people but I persevered and after hours of queuing I was shown inside a room where we had to pair up with another person. We all had to say something which would make us stand out about ourselves. I, of course, said I used to be married to Charlie Bronson. I can't remember what my partner said about herself but we both went through to the next round of interviews. In this round you went in to the interview room on your own and sat in front of a camera with two producers sitting opposite you and asked you to say something about yourself. I told them about failing my driving test 3 times and deciding to buy a three wheeler car and painting it bright pink with the registration number IRE 1because at the time I don't think you had to have passed your driving test to drive one. I said I thought I could make the three wheeler car really popular! If you passed that stage, the next step in the interview procedure was to go into a large hall with everyone else who had reached that stage and fill in loads of forms. You also had to sign a secrecy document, you were not allowed to tell anyone at all you had auditioned to be on the show. By the end of all that it was early evening and everyone was told they could go home but they asked me to go back again on Sunday morning to do another couple of interviews. At this point I was feeling quite confident. I kept thinking what good fun it would be to be on Big Brother!

When Sunday came, off I went back to Manchester on the train again. I took a big pink rabbit called The Wave with me, and it was big, it used to ripple up and down like a wave, and yes it was thick, in fact it was quite huge! The third part of the interview took part inside a sort of tent where you sat on your own. Right in front of you was a camera with a long lens. I sat there for about 15 minutes wondering what was going to happen next. I started to get a bit fidgety and was feeling the sides of the tent then I got up and stared down the camera to see if I could see anything. I heard someone laughing outside the tent and re-alised at this point that Davina McCall and another producer were sitting there, although I couldn't see them. Then a loud voice spoke to me, a man's voice, and said 'Big Brother want s to know what you are doing holding a big bright pink dildo in your hand?' I replied that it was not a dildo but a vibrator a Pink Rabbit, and showed them what it did. I couldn't see them at this point but they could watch me through the camera . I told them that I had recently sold one of these rabbits to an 80 year old woman when I was in work at Ann Summers. Then a voice said' Irene, Big Brother just wants to be sick into the waste bin'. After they asked me a couple more questions I was told to leave the tent and a crew member would take me to the next interview which was called the 'The Waiting Room'. I went into another large room which had a few settees and chairs scattered around. There were other people there who had also passed the previous interviews and some producers too. They told us to start chatting to other people in the room. I had my Pink Rabbit with me still and it proved a good talking point. I kept asking people to have a feel of it and if they refused I put it against their arms which made everyone laugh, including the producers. After about an hour in that room we were taken by a crew member to collect our coats and warned again not to tell anyone where we had been. They said they would contact us if we were not successful.

At this point I was quite optimistic and started to think that I may be chosen to appear on Big Brother, I was so excited. After a few weeks there was no phone call to say I was unsuccessful so I thought, Oh yeah, I'm going to be on Big Brother! You see, they wouldn't contact you until the last minute if you were chosen - for privacy reasons. So that's why I was so optimistic. But as you know, I didn't go on Big Brother. I was never told the reason why but the only thing I can think of was that unbeknown to me Mick's film called Bronson was about to be released in cinemas and that could have been the reason for not being selected. Your guess is as good as mine. God, I was soooo disappointed. Never mind, hey!

Chapter Ten: More Spirits

As the years went by my second husband and I were not getting on too well; in fact he really did get on my nerves. I soon found a way to make me feel so less stressed with Mr X. I had made pancakes and had dropped Mr Xs on the floor. Now at that time my kitchen extension was half finished which meant part of the floor was unfinished and covered in little stones and bits of cement. It was also very dusty and dirty by the cooker but I picked the pancake up and took out a few of the bigger stones, wiped it with a cloth and served it up to him. Mr X ate every bit of it, dust and all because it would have been such a shame to waste it I gave it to him. About a week afterwards we had another big row; even though we had many rows I always cooked an evening meal for us all. I thought it was mean not to cook for him just because of the arguments, although I had friends who wouldn't cook for their partners. I remember one day in particular we were having pork chops. I popped out of the kitchen for a few minutes leaving the raw chops out on a plate on the work top. When I came back into the kitchen our cat Gimley had taken a chop off the plate and was eagerly devouring it on the floor amongst the dust and stones. It looked as though he was really enjoying it ! Naughty Gimley I said. At this point Mike came into the kitchen and said oh mum, you'll have to throw it away now. No love I said it'll be fine, Mr X will really enjoy it!

As time went by I often use this practice to release my stress levels with Mr X. I once mixed all the gravy up with the dirty washing up water and poured it over Mr X's meal. He didn't even notice but God I felt so much less stressed knowing what I'd done. Another time Gimley had jumped up onto the kitchen table whilst I was serving up our dinner. He picked up a nice slice of lamb from a plate and proceeded to eat it on the kitchen floor. Again I picked it up wiped off the bigger stones, poured gravy all over it and put it on the plate ready for Mr X to tuck into. When Mr X came to the table and started eating his meal, poor Gimley sat next to him mewing as if to say 'hey, you're eating my dinner'.

The rows continued and so did my stress relief measures. It really worked well for me because to see Mr X eating something I had done something to made all my stress disappear as if by magic. I should point out here that no animals or people were hurt during my stress relief practices. Oh well, hey, never mind.

Just thought that if anyone reading this would like a nice cup of tea or anything to eat at my house you are very welcome to pop in anytime! Anyway, all's well that ends well. Just wondering if any of you reading this have guessed who Mr X is ???

During the time Mr X and I were not getting on, in fact I think it was when he'd moved back in with his parents, I noticed I was having a lot more visits from spirits – male spirits actually. In particular, there was one spirit who used to come and visit me more and more frequently. In fact, in the end he used

Me aged 6 years

Thicket Ford, Number 1 Sandy Lane

Family photo with me in the bottom left

Mick, Mungo Jerry style!

The only photo I have left of Mick and I together

With baby Michael

In the garden with Michael

Another in the garden with Michael

Michael aged 7 years

Mum, Michael and his little sister and brother

Michael at home aged 2

Michael off to go fishing

Me with Leicia

Michael with his catch

Mum, Michael and I in 1984

Mum, me and my ex mother-in-law

Me (left) at a family wedding

London, August 2010

At the races

Happy birthday to me!

Me with the bike my workmates bought me

Tom Hardy with Mick's mum Eira

Night out with the girls

Michael meeting his dad for the
first time after 26 years

Mike and I, taken after
the documentary

Paula and I waving to the fans after
appearing on Loose Women

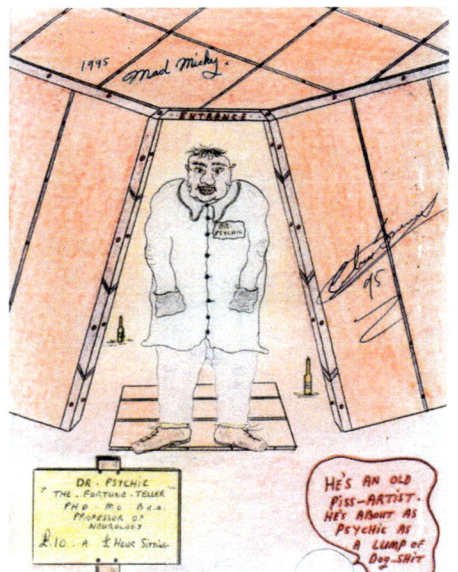

Above: 'Mad Micky' from 1995 on a card
Below: Mick's message on reverse

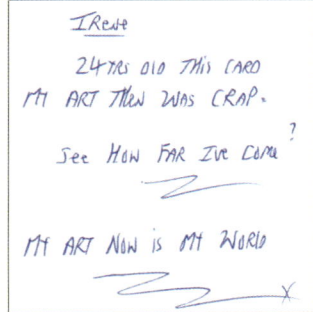

Uncle Dick

NOT A BAD SHOPPER FOR AN O-AP

Irene

One of Mick's cards

**Above and Left:
One of Mick's
canteen receipts**

IRene
HEALTH is EveryThing
PRICELESS.
WiThout iT Your Fucked up.

IM COMING OUT To TURN iT ARound
AND
ENJOY WHATS LEFT of LIFE
iN COMFORT

Me at work

Mick's positive
about the future

Another card from Mick

Charlie cleared of jail assault

BRITAIN'S most violent inmate Charles Bronson has been cleared of trying to bite off the nose of a prison governor.

Bronson, 65, admitted whistling the theme to The Great Escape before launching himself at Mark Docherty in HMP Wakefield.

Mr Docherty had barred him from looking at photos of his wedding to former Coronation Street actress Paula Williamson.

But the notorious armed robber claimed: "I'm as innocent as Donald Trump" and accused Mr Docherty of telling "porky pies" about the ferocity of the attack.

During a four-day trial at Leeds Crown Court Bronson, who represented himself, said he would "never have bitten the governor's nose off". He added: "I'm a vegetarian."

And he told jurors: "For once in my life, I really am an innocent man."

As he was cleared of GBH yesterday Bronson, who appeared via videolink from HMP Frankland in Durham, began dancing and waving his arms.

He told Judge Tom Bayliss QC: "British justice system – best in the world. Thank you."

I punched the glass. Blood shot out like a fountain. I was on the edge of insanity

Chance for Bronson?

PRISON hardman Charles Bronson continues to be one of Britain's most fascinating characters.

Our revelations today about his will – that he plans to have tattooed on his back – confirm his standing.

But you have to wonder why he is still in jail after 46 years.

Bronson has never killed anybody and his life sentence was for offences he committed while incarcerated.

No doubt he has been a very violent man in his time. The prison officers he took hostage will feel strongly that he does not deserve any sympathy.

So, too, will the terrified art teacher who was also taken hostage for criticising Bronson's drawings.

But there are mass murderers, multiple rapists and jihadi bombers at large in this country, having completed only part of their sentences. Some have gone on to commit further evil crimes.

Why is it that Bronson has remained locked up for so long?

There may be good reasons and we do not advocate his release for the sake of it. If there is a chance that he could reoffend, he must stay there.

Yet it is surely time for a review?

And we deserve to know why Charles Bronson is treated worse than serial killers and terrorists.

MAD, BAD AND

DANGEROUS

BRONSON NICKED IN KNICKERS

Lifer: I wore wife's frillies on a raid.. it gave coppers a big shock!

Get me a cuppa or I'll eat one of the Iraqis

Some of the headlines Mick has made over the years

to visit me nearly every night. I was so scared, I was terrified to go to sleep. I used to leave my TV on all night and all the lights on and try and read all through the night so I wouldn't drop off to sleep. If any of you has had one of these visitations you will know that the spirit is much more powerful when you are asleep as your mind is open to their energy and they can connect much more easily to you. You try to wake up and shout out to family members but it goes unheard; as if there is a force preventing you from awakening and the more you struggle the more energy the spirit receives from your force and he just gets stronger and stronger. The spirit man who came to visit me I originally thought was the old man spirit we used to see with the old woman spirit and the little boy spirit who was always on his knees praying. The male spirit never lay on top of me again trying to kiss me with his foul breath but instead he came behind me when I was lying down . He used to put his arms around my waist and pull me against him. My God, he was so strong and his arms were vicelike and still to this day I can feel the shape of his penis against my back. It was so, so bad I just couldn't free myself. I used to look over my shoulder and ask him 'Who are you, who are you?' He never spoke and I never knew what he looked like but I felt him very strongly and it took me longer and longer to force my mind away from him and be able to open my eyes.

It got so bad, I hadn't been sleeping properly, I was worn out most of the time and absolutely terrified, that my daughter said to me 'Mum, you can't carry on like this, you'll have to try and get rid of the spirit'. It so happened she knew of a friend of one of her work colleagues at the hospital who had helped a young mother and son get rid of a little girl spirit who had thought they were her mother and brother. She gave me this lady's number; I had to ring her from the house where the visitations took place for it to work. It was a Friday night and I was in on my own when I made that phone call. Her name was Jan and, almost as soon as she spoke to me, she fell to her knees. She said 'yes, you have a man with you, he appears to be a small man but in fact he'd had a bad accident and lost both his legs below his knees. He doesn't want to harm you but he used to be a bit of a womaniser before his accident and he misses that and just wants to hug you'. 'You what' I said, 'he can go and hug off! I don't want him anywhere near me, I don't want him coming nearly every night 'hugging' me. She told me that the old man and woman spirit in the house were there to protect me. It all made sense to me then. No wonder he had such strong arms and he was the spirit I thought was a young boy praying. My God though, why did I have to have him instead of some gorgeous, young hunk wanting to hug me! Oh well, never mind hey.

Jan told me over the phone that he would not be hard to get rid off but said to give her half an hour and she would do whatever she had to do to try and get rid of him. She told me not to be scared but she was going to send a couple of spirits to me to take him away. 'You won't see them' she said 'but you may feel them but they won't harm you, they are good spirits'. Oh my God, I was scared. I put all the lights on in the house and opened all the windows and doors, front and back. I texted my daughter who was at a cottage in Bala in Wales at the time and told her what was happening. She kept on the phone for about 15 minutes and do you know what? I was so cold I was shaking then I felt calm then cold again . I just knew this was the spirits floating all over the house, backwards and forwards.

I kept saying to Leicia, 'oh, they're here now, I'm so cold' then I'd say ' they've gone upstairs now', then 'they're back again in the room with me'. Leicia was doing her best to keep me calm. Then, I suddenly knew it was over – the spirits were finally out of the house. I put the phone down and saw a text from Jan saying the spirits had indeed left the house. The relief I felt was fantastic but then the following night I had another horrible dream. I was in a gondola in Italy. I had just left my friends at a bar and was alone in the gondola with the gondolier. He had a bright red scarf tied around his waist which he then took off and tied it around me and pulled me to him. I tried to wake up which I eventually managed to do and out of the corner of my eye I could see what looked like a whirlpool of water rising higher and higher away from me.

I was worried the spirit had come back to me so I contacted Jan again and she told me not to worry, he's gone now and he won't come back. I believe that the whirlpool of water was in fact his spirit rising away from me and out of my life. I hope so anyway. It was so lovely to be able to go to bed and not be too afraid to sleep. My daughter told me afterwards that whilst we were talking on the phone, she was feeling exactly the same emotions as I was. Ohhh, spooky!

I had a couple of weeks of really peaceful sleep after that. Then one night I tried to open my eyes because my bed was rocking from side to side. It was a struggle to keep myself from falling out but felt as though my bed wanted me to fall out of it. After that experience I rang Jan again and asked her to find out what was going on. She said she would investigate and get back to me when she had an answer. Guess what? She told me it was a male spirit just passing through who had made a quick visit to me. Why me, I wondered? Am I on some spiritual dating website or what?

Never sleep on a cactus: Charlie Salvador

Chapter Eleven: Ian

I used to go out into town on a Friday night with a group of friends (and what great times we had!). It was on one of these nights out that I met this man who was working in Chester. He was from Yorkshire and was an electrical engineer whose job took him around the country and abroad. We started dating, his name was Ian, and eventually I went to live with him in his beautiful home in Yorkshire. I had to leave my job at Ethel Austins and say goodbye to all my lovely work colleagues. It was so hard, I loved them all and we had had such good times together but also Ian was becoming very important to me too. Little did I know at the time that I would go from selling old ladies' big knickers and mens' underpants to selling sex toys and sex aids. I would never have believed it if I'd been told at the time. How weird, hey, how your life can change in the blink of an eye.

Ian had two children who were a lot younger than mine; my children had all grown up and had lives of their own but Ian's children were still both at school. Ian, his kids and I used to have some fab days, we had so many laughs when we were all out together.

Ian was also very generous, and I mean very generous! He used to take me to Morrisons in Middlesbrough, which was about a 30 minute drive from his lovely bungalow in Nunthorpe, to get the groceries. He used to say put whatever you like into the trolley and don't worry about the cost. I had a little grandson at this time so I used to put all sorts of baby things into it as well as things I needed and sometimes the checkout total would be £300 - £400 at a time. Oh, it was so good. He also used to take me to designer shops in town and buy me anything I wanted. If I couldn't make up my mind about the colour or style he would say 'Don't worry, I'll buy you both of them'. I've actually still got all my designer clothes from those shopping trips but, sadly, don't get the opportunity to wear them any more.

He always took me on fantastic holidays and I have lots of lovely photos and memories of them all, especially Egypt. We took a day trip to Cairo on one of our holidays from where we were staying on a small plane. It was such a fun-filled day! We did everything , we went to the mosques, we went to the pyramids, we went to the museum – we packed so much in. We went for a meal then a cruise down the Nile. The captain of the boat told Ian he wanted to buy me! Luckily Ian didn't want to sell me. Our lunch was in a beautiful palace just by the pyramids. Some amazing experiences and sights. I just love Egypt!.

Another trip I went on with Ian was to Paris for the weekend. That was so good too. He showed me the Moulin Rouge and the district where all the sex shops are and the red light district too. We went into one of the sex shops because, at that time, thigh length boots were coming into fashion and I wanted some. This particular sex shop had some fantastic, red, thigh high boots on display and I wanted them. The shop also had a lipstick which vibrated. I was shocked as I'd never seen sex toys before. Little did I know that not long afterwards I myself would be working in Ann Summers selling similar sex toys and sex aids! Anyway back in the shop, he wouldn't buy the boots for me because he said if I wore them and then stood around waiting for him I'd get picked up for soliciting! He said I'd look like a hooker. I was so disappointed as he'd never said no to me before. But I DID GET HIM TO CHANGE HIS MIND! The following day we went straight back to the shop but unfortunately the shop was shut and that was the end of that. The story has a happy ending though as a couple of weeks later Ian did buy me some beautiful soft, black leather thigh boots from a shop in Liverpool and I loved them.

Ian used to work away a lot, both abroad and all over the country here. He used to go to work early on a Monday morning and not come back home until Friday afternoon. I used to hate Monday mornings when the time came for him to leave so I decided to get a little part-time job to pass away the time. Ian had printed out some CVs for me and I took the bus to Middlesbrough and left my CV in some of the clothes shops and boutiques. I'd run out of CVs when I came across an Ann Summers shop advertising for sales staff. Oh no, I thought I haven't got a CV to leave and I don't want to get the bus all the way back home to pick up some more so I retraced my steps and went back into the last shop I'd left a CV in, I think it was Dorothy Perkins, and asked if they'd mind giving me it back. They gave it back to me and I handed it in at Ann Summers and subsequently got an interview with them a couple of days later.

During the interview, we were sitting in a little staff room (Ann Summers in Middlesbrough is quite a small shop) and I looked around the room and saw boxes that had just been delivered. On the front of one of them I saw the words Snake Trousers printed and assumed it was because of Justin Timberlake who was supposed to be like a snake. You can use your imagination to see where the snake fits! To be honest I was shocked, I was really, really shocked! Then I was shown into an area of the store which was full of rabbits, big ones, little ones, pink ones, silver ones, black ones! Again I was in shock. These were not the cute rabbits that eat lettuce, these were proper vibrators, sex toys which seemed to do everything a lot better than a man could do!

You can see at this point, even though I had often shopped in Ann Summers in Liverpool and Chester, I never went anywhere near the sex toys or even glanced at the naughty novelties. I used to like looking at the pretty underwear and nighties, so I'm not lying when I say I was in shock when I saw the range of goods on sale in Ann Summers! God bless my mum, she never knew what I did for a living when I worked there even though she often asked me what sort of shop I worked in. 'Oh, it's a lovely underwear shop' I would tell her. She would have been horrified if she had known. Oh well, never mind, hey. Our manageress there was called Rosie, she's still there now and the other girls there were all lovely. We all got on very well together and had a lot of laughs. There used to be a man come into the shop, always wearing white shorts and white sports socks. He would run into the shop, make right for the bottom where all the sex toys were and jump up and down on the spot in front of a Vibro Ring cock ring. This particular one used to amuse him and it was always this one he used to jump up and down in front of. Then he would turn around and run straight back out again without saying a word to anyone. Ah, bless him, he was harmless (well I think he was anyway!)

Another time a man ran into the shop shouting 'Sex, sex, I want sex'. He ran up to Rosie the manageress still shouting 'Sex, sex'; she turned to him and in a very stern voice told him 'Sex, sex, not in my shop, leave please' which he did without another word.

I remember in the changing room at the Middlesbrough shop there was only one key to the door and we always kept it on the outside of the door which we kept locked until a customer wanted to try something on. One particular time I showed a lady in to try something on and locked the door and pocketed the key. In the meantime, I was asked by another customer about something in the front of the shop. Off I went with her sorting through things for her size then after about half an hour the manageress came up to me and said 'Oh Irene, you locked a customer in the changing room!' I felt awful, the poor woman! Oh well, never mind.

On another occasion I was dusting the light fittings with a feather duster. The next thing I know is that all the alarms go off and the feather duster has gone up in flames! Oh well, all's well that ends well. No, I'm afraid the Middlesbrough girls will never forget me but they did love me really, honestly!

When I first met Ian he was divorced and had bought an old bungalow which he had renovated. I helped him by picking the curtains, furniture and colour schemes. One night when we were in bed I asked him who the old man and woman were standing at the end of the bed. This really freaked Ian out because, unbeknown to me, he had bought this house from the family of an old couple who used to live there. Freaky, hey?

I did find it very difficult living so far away from my family and couldn't always go home to visit because of the shifts I was working. Rosie could see that this was bothering me and we had a few chats about it. She said to me 'Irene, I know you're missing your family, are you happy to carry on working here ?'. She said I should have a good think about it and if I decided to leave Ian and go back home to the Wirral, she would make sure that I would be transferred to the Liverpool or Chester Ann Summers shop. She explained that she thought I had such a unique way of selling that she didn't want the company to lose me. I would eventually do this, but before I made a decision the area manager presented me with a lovely certificate proclaiming me the 'North East's Most Magical Temp' and a gift card for £20 plus a large box of chocolates. I was so made up I cried.

As time went on I found myself increasingly missing my family back home. I started to go home every other week, but when I left Ian I cried and when I left my family I cried. I just couldn't win. My elderly mum was living on her own and missed me. Whenever I rang her she'd ask me if I was coming home that week and if I said no, not this week she would just put the phone down. Also, my little grandson would ask me on the phone when I was coming home and he'd get upset if I said not for another week. I was torn, it was so hard but I started coming home more often and for longer periods of time. Ian wasn't happy at all about this, he kept saying 'you've got to make your mind up where you want to live – here with me or back home in Heswall'. In the end Heswall won and I eventually came back to live in Heswall for good.

Leaving that Middlesbrough Ann Summers shop was quite upsetting for me. I'd come to love Rosie and the girls but needs must. I have so many wonderful memories of my time there and we still exchange Christmas cards, etc. Ahhh!

I remember my daughter saying to me at the time 'Mum, never mind, you're back in the real world now', meaning no more designer clothes, no more fabulous holidays unless I could afford to pay for them myself. And yes, I do miss all that luxury living. Oh well!!

Sadly, Ian has since died, God bless him. But he has been in touch with me vias a medium with my mum and dad who are both now in spirit. He told me we are soulmates and that when I die he is coming to get me and we'll be together for eternity. How lovely is that! I may not have a partner now but I will have one in the spirit world when I pass too. That gives me hope.

Chapter Twelve: Back Home

When I was transferred to the Liverpool Ann Summers from Middlesbrough I soon fitted in and became friendly with all the girls. It was situated very near to a pub and we used to get a lot of men in who were inebriated. They'd had a few drinks to give them the courage to actually come into our shop. In fact, I do find that it always seems to be the men who are more embarrassed than the women, Gid bless their little hearts. Right opposite our shop was Matthew Street where the Cavern club is where the Beatles and Cilla Black used to perform. Guess what, our shop was where the Beatles used to sing and practice, downstairs. We had a massive room that was used as a stock room plus an office and toilets also. Nearly every time someone went downstairs to the stock room they could hear the rustling of newspapers and quite often the lights used to go out in the toilets and quite often in the office. Upon arrival in the morning the manageress would often find the viewing angle of the camera would have changed and sometimes she would find the fridge door was wide open. Weird hey! But that's not all; sometimes the doors downstairs would open and close on their own so if you happened to be down there it would frighten the life out of you. We soon came to love our spirit though and found out is was Brian Epstein, God bless his soul. We found a photo of him and one of the girls made it into a poster which we put up downstairs and whenever we walked past it we would say 'Hi Brian'. In the office we had a large poster of Brian Epstein signing up Cilla Black – amazing! We used to get groups of foreign tourists with their tour guides wanting to go downstairs to see where the Beatles used to practice but obviously they were not allowed.

Sadly, we had to leave that old building as it needed renovation and the shop moved to Liverpool One. We were all sad to leave Brian and said our goodbyes to him and told him he was very welcome to come with us to Liverpool One store but he must have decided against it! He must have wanted to stay with his memories. That wasn't the end of a spirit being with us though. This time it was a man in a black cape and black top hat. I'm afraid we didn't like him at all, he was very scary. He always liked to stand by the vibrators and sex toys. Sometimes he would turn them on and they would be jumping about on the shelves. Spooky! One Halloween, I told some customers I was demonstrating to , not to worry when the toys started to vibrate on their own, as it was only the ghost. I'm sure they thought I was joking. Oh well, never mind hey.

Another weird experience I had in that shop was about a box. I needed to pop into the store room for something and said to the girls if I'm not back in half an hour come and get me. I was joking, but what is it about those words when I say them? Eeeh, is it a secret code to the spirit world? I went through the door and made my way to the stock room. As I approached it, I could hear the sound of cardboard being ripped apart. I stopped, listened and wondered what it was as I knew there was no-one in there. As I stood in the doorway, I saw the big box we used to store sale items in. It was empty but was moving up and down slowly, right in front of me. At the same time, I could still hear the ripping sound. I turned round and ran into the manager's office. He was sitting at his desk working on his computer.' Tom, Tom' I shouted 'he's back'. 'Who' asked Tom. 'The ghost' I said. Tom was not at all psychic, in fact he didn't believe in anything like that. He just thought I was being my normal, slightly weird, self. Give him his due he did say 'Let's have a look on the security cameras then' and sure enough there I was standing in the doorway staring at this large cardboard box moving up and down right in front of me. The odd thing was though that the moment I turned around to run away the box stopped moving. It was all caught on camera. No, it wasn't me being weird, it really happened, honestly. Tom was amazed. He completely changed his opinion about spirits after that. He said there was no way the box could have moved by itself. So Tom is now also a believer. We kept the footage for a long time, it was quite a conversation starter alright!

One night when we were closing the shop, we were all stood at the tills when one of the girls said she felt cold. I said I did too and another girl also felt cold and the hairs on our arms were standing on end. Oh, it's the ghost we said so I said out loud 'Look if you're here with us now, give us a sign'. The next thing was all the door alarms went off. This really freaked us out. We all ran into the back, got our coats and bags ready to leave and then as we passed the sex toys they all started to go off. We ran to the door in fright. This spirit seemed quite threatening, I don't think he was a good spirit.

That was still not the end of the spirit stories though. We left that shop and moved upstairs to another shop in Liverpool One, where we are to this day. I'll tell you about that later on.

I am trying to write this book in the order that events happened, but I'm not too good with dates at all! Come on I've had three different birthdays, is it any wonder I'm not, and even now when I know my true birthday, my children always say to me every year 'what day are you having your birthday on this year, mum?' Somehow it always seems to be a Friday. I love a Friday, don't you?!.

Another funny incident happened whilst I was at work in this shop. It was a Saturday and I had a couple in – they were young, 18 or 19. They were so sweet. They were looking for a beginner's sex toy, not too big for the girl. I showed them what we had available and they seemed really pleased. I also decided to show them a lube (lubricant) called white satin. It's a lovely lube, you can also use it for massages. I pointed out to them the lovely feel of it when you put it on the toy. Lubes actually makes the toys feel so much silkier. I also said to them I'd better make sure I point the nozzle in the right direction because every time I had squeezed it earlier, the lube came out in the wrong direction. Just wanted to point out that lube with a toy is like having strawberries and cream but without it it's like just having the strawberries. Well I always say that anyway – if you get my meaning? Anway, I squirted the lube, a white lotion, onto the toy but oh no, I missed again! The lube went all over the lad's trousers around the groin area! The poor bloke was in shock but his girlfriend was in hysterics laughing. I think it's true to say they will never forget the first time they went into Ann Summers! Bless them! Anyway, it's a fun shop, isn't it, so never mind hey!

Sometimes we get some really lovely customers in, we always have lovely chats and laughs with them and get quite attached to some, they are so lovely. When they are like that it makesour day, we feel so blessed we have been able to help them and they are so happy with their goods. It is a great feeling, it really is. Obviously, we do get the odd customer who can be very rude to us, even though we are doing our best to be nice and helpful to them. Two of these said customers were really rude to a few of us in the shop. When they eventually left the shop with their items, they stood in the doorway and pretended to point a gun at us. Not a real gun obviously, they just used their fingers to imitate a gun and went 'bang, bang' at us. Luckily, the percentage of this type of customer is low and all the lovely customers more than make up for them.

When I'm selling the toys I always do my best to make it fun. Sometimes, when we get a really good new toy in I demonstrate (as in show) it and start to sing Tina Turner's 'its simply the best, better than all the rest' and this usually puts the customers at ease and brings a smile to their face. We also get a lot of very shy customers in the shop and we all do our best to make them feel at ease. I mean, you wouldn't show these customers a big vibrator, especially if they are first timers to the toys; you do have to be discreet at times. I love it when some of these customers later come back in and thank me for my recommendation and say it was perfect for him or her. That gives you a nice 'buzz' too!

We also get a lot of students in; Liverpool has a large student population. Most of them are great but occasionally we get groups of students in who just want to show off to their mates in front of the girls and start throwing the toys around and acting stupidly and sticking the dildos (not vibrating) with the suction bases onto other toys. They can be very annoying as it puts regular customers off. One group of students were really getting on my nerves. I kept calm until they turned on everything to vibrate and they thought it was hilarious. I said to them 'oh boys, I think you're in the wrong toy shop, Disney is downstairs'. They left then without another word!

Ah, I remember another lovely old couple who came into the toy section one day. The man picked up a big body wand. It is for massaging but obviously you can use it wherever you want. It's shaped like a microphone and a lot of the men on seeing this in the shop immediately pretend to sing down it. Anyway, the old gentleman pretended to sing down it and I thought 'here we go again' but Oh my God, he had the most amazing voice! He sang an entire Elvis Presley song and he had a voice just like Elvis – he even did the ahaha bits. I said to his wife he should be singing professionally and she told me he did use to sing in his younger days. In the end he sang another Elvis song to the girls at

the till. Ahh, that's a lovely memory of his voice, God bless him.
When some of the shy customers are looking for a toy I usually say to them
things like 'this one is really good, I have one myself' but do I really have one of
those toys? Mmmm.

I travel backwards and forwards to work by bus. I don't drive – I could
never pass my driving test. I took it three times and at the last one I was in a
right panic, my feet were bouncing up and down on the pedals. The examiner
was sitting sideways in his seat with one arm on the dashboard and the other
on the back of the seat. Why he chose to sit like that I've no idea but he did look
a bit anxious. He asked me to pull up and get out of the car, stretch my legs and
take some deep breaths for 10 minutes, which I did. I got back into the car to
continue the test. I wound the window down, stuck my head out and said 'I'm
fine now' and then reversed the car up onto the pavement. Luckily there was
nobody on the path and I hadn't run anyone over so everything was fine. We
got back to Birkenhead Test Centre and the examiner told me that I had passed!
No telling a lie, I didn't pass I'm afraid and third time was definitely not lucky for
me. I don't think driving is for me anyway. Whenever my second husband gave
me a driving lesson, I used to think to myself 'I could drive right into that wall'
or ' I could let go of the steering wheel just to see what would happen' Scary
business indeed.

I do enjoy my bus journeys into work though. I always sit at the back.
I have a good reason for doing this as it means no-one can sit behind me. Believe me, if you know what I know and see what goes on the bus , you would do
the same. You get to know all of your fellow travellers, bless their little hearts.

If anyone reading this knows me, you will know that I'm really being
quite sarcastic. There's a bloke who often gets on my bus in Liverpool. As he
gets on he looks to see if there are any women on the bus, particularly if there
are any women wearing skirts. I'm not kidding, he makes it so obvious ; he
walks up and down the bus looking in all directions. If he can't sit next to the
skirt wearing woman, he sits as close as he can and constantly looks at her.
Eehh I've watched him so many times. I always wear trousers but I still put my
bags on my knees whenever he gets on and give him warning looks to make
sure he doesn't sit next to me. If there are no skirt wearing women on the bus
he gets off at the next stop and gets another bus and repeats the whole process
again. Weird man.

I think my really favourite travelling companion is the seat wetting old
gentleman. He always gets on in Birkenhead and gets off after a few stops. He
always leaves a lovely little reminder on the seat he's been sitting on, usually
a seat at the front of the bus. BEWARE! A couple of times we have had to tell
passengers getting on 'Don't sit there!' Honestly!

Another day this well dressed, middle aged lady got on the bus. She's
quite a regular, she usually tries to engage the other passengers in conversation, which is the last thing you want to do after a long day at work. I'm always

too tired to talk; I just like to sit there thinking and stopping myself from nodding off with the movement of the bus. Anyway she was already sat at the front of the bus when the seat wetting man got on at Birkenhead. She said to him in a dead loud voice ' oh love, sit here by me, I'll let you sit on the window side'. I was thinking 'oh no, you're definitely going to regret this'. The old man's stop came and the lady got up to let him get past her then at were he'd been sitting. You should have heard her! She started shouting for all to hear 'He's weed all over my coat, it's wringing wet, he's weed all over it'. I had to stop myself from laughing, I knew this would happen. She then proceeded to tell the driver all about the wet seat then took herself off to sit somewhere else, all the time moaning about it to anyone who would listen. Oh, I do love the bus!

On another occasion, a gentleman got on the bus again in Liverpool. He sat in the front, on the side seat just behind the driver. Anyway, when we got to Birkenhead bus station, the driver stopped the bus and said something to this man. I thought he was asking him to show his bus pass but the man didn't acknowledge the driver at all. The driver then repeated it and still got no response. He then said to the man 'I'm not going anywhere until you get off this bus'. I shouted to the man 'Show him your bus pass' because I was tired and wanted to get home. Two students were sitting a few seats in front of me; they turned round and said to me 'The driver isn't asking to see his bus pass, he's asking the man to get off the bus because he's covered in shit'. They were the exact words. Oh my God, eehh. Still the man sat there without saying anything. The driver than rang the bus depot's security number and two security guards got on the bus and asked the man to get off. Finally he got up and got off the bus with them. The driver then tied a roll of tickets around the side seat so no-one would sit there. As the bus went past the man and security guards I did everything I could to keep my eyes averted from the man but in those situations which are really sickening, you do look; something just makes you look and believe me I really wished I hadn't looked. I'll save you a description of what I saw. Ah, aren't I kind!

At this point I do really want to point out that you do get some really nice fellow travellers on the bus, too and I have become friends with quite a few of them. One thing I don't love about the bus though is the germs. A lot of passengers don't like the windows open, so the glass becomes covered in mist then runs down the windows making the bus very clammy. I absolutely hate that. I always try to open a window and if another passenger shuts it I give them one of my dirty looks – if looks could kill look!

One morning I was on my way to work. This time I was not in my usual seat at the back for some reason and a couple of students, a girl and a boy, got on and sat right behind me. I had the window open by my seat and the next thing I know they shut the window. I re-opened it then the girl started to shut it again. I just caught sight of her arm . I said to her 'I've just opened that window' and she said to me it's freezing in here so I told her to sit elsewhere on the bus away from the window. She told me she wanted to stay sitting at the back. I'm afraid I then said to her 'Well, I'm sorry but that window is staying open. Look at all the windows full of germs, everyone's breathing them all in'. She said to me 'You should drive then and not get on the bus'. I don't drive anyway. She didn't say anything else and left the window open. When they both got off in Birkenhead, they started to walk up the stairs. As the bus went past them they looked at me and I put my two fingers up at them! Oh dear, I think I shocked them.

Because of all these germs which float around the bus by people sneezing and coughing and whatever my hygienic fellow travellers do, I have to wear a mask. I always have done for years or wrapped a scarf around my mouth and nose. I used to get a lot of double takes from passengers getting on the bus. I had one man saying to me 'who are you hiding from?' Another one said to me 'What do you know that we don't?' Bear in mind this was pre Covid before people had to wear masks. You see, I did say that I was psychic! Sometimes you just have to do what you have to do.

Chapter Thirteen: Bronson

Many years ago when Mick was in prison, I received some legal documents to sign about a film they wanted to make about Mick. They wanted my permission for someone to portray me, but on reading the contract and getting my brother-in-law to read it too and explain to me what it entailed – it was all in legal jargon and I didn't have a clue what it all meant – I decided not to sign it and never sent the contract back to them. There was a rumour at the time that Michael Winner wanted to produce the film although I didn't hear anything about that afterwards.

Years later, I was told that Tom Hardy was going to play Mick in the film. I wasn't consulted about anything in the film even though they had an actress playing me in it. When the film was released and about to be shown in cinemas around the country, a couple of the girls from work went upstairs at the cinema in Liverpool One to look at the advertising posters of coming films. When they came back they told me that Mick's film Bronson was advertised and that there was a big poster of Mick and on his arm they said he had a heart tattoo with an arrow through it saying Irene. Ah, I was touched, even though I didn't know when or how Mick could have had that tattoo done because when we were together Mick didn't have any tattoos.

I didn't go to the cinema to see the film, I felt too emotional, but when it came out on DVD an ex-boyfriend played it on the tv as a surprise for me. It did upset me and I couldn't bring myself to watch it all. All the violence against Mick by the heavy mob was so upsetting for me so I've never actually watched it to the end.

Now Tom Hardy is a fabulous actor and he performed the script he was given really well but, to be honest, the film did nothing at all for Mick. It portrayed him as a maniac clown, there was so much fabrication in it and not enough of the real Bronson portrayed in it. Also, they seemed to have got a lot of the part of myself and a girl who went to visit him in prison, mixed up. I can quite honestly say that I have never, ever been tall nor have I ever worked in a chip shop and to be perfectly honest I don't think Mick has either. They portrayed the girlfriend as someone petite and dark like myself and the actress playing me wasn't at all like me.

There was also a scene in the film were Mick covered his naked body in paint but the true version of this was that he did get covered in paint, but only after I had painted our bath bright turquoise. Mick had come in from work and gone upstairs and jumped in the bath before I had a chance to tell him the paint wasn't dry and all could hear was him shouting from upstairs 'I'm covered in paint Irene, I'm covered in paint'! I couldn't stop laughing at the time and eventually Mick saw the joke also and I must say that his olive skin did look lovely with the bright turquoise paint, he really suited it! Ah, bless him.

Also, in the film they showed the actress playing me wearing one of those aprons that your granny or great granny would wear in the olden days,

holding Mike and standing watching Mick cleaning a gun.' What!!!?' I can cat-
egorically say I never wore an apron, I was always dressed dead trendy, and I
have never, ever seen Mick holding a gun. Never!!!

During this time Mike and I found out what was really happening to
Mick in prison. It was so upsetting and worrying for us both; it just went on and
on and on and still to this day it's going on. I wanted Mick out of prison so much,
especially for Mike. He had always really missed his dad and needed him in his
life – not in prison. Even though I had remarried and Mike was getting older,
the effects were still really affecting us both. You're at a loss, what can you do?
Nothing, nothing at all it's all out of your hands and because Mick had become
Bronson, it was just getting harder and harder for us both to come to terms with
it. A living nightmare - I wouldn't wish the experience on anyone.

The authorities all thought 'oh well, we'll keep Mick in forever and
make his life hell'. But do they think about his family – his son and his elderly
mother who are suffering because of it? No, of course they don't. There is
never any peace of mind for them at all, for years and years and years. We just
want him out and now so many people are finding out the truth about Mick, the
real reasons why he is still being kept in prison will come out. I have always and
will always support Mick through thick and thin. I will always have his back - I
know what has gone on in there and have done from the very beginning. It's
heart-breaking. They have tried again and again to break him; how he's survived such treatment and for so long is a credit to him. He is so positive and he
knows, as I do, that he is coming out either at the end of this year or definitely
next year.

People do really think that he's some sort of mad serial killer. A lot of
people have said to me over the years 'He's a murderer isn't he, that's why he's
still in prison after all these years?'. They think he's another Hannibal Lecter
or Charles Manson but ,no, Mick has never killed anyone, or raped women
or hurt children. He's never blown people up like a terrorist, he's not a paedo-
phile, all crimes which do deserve a long imprisonment. All the bad people who
do commit these terrible crimes are all too often let out back onto the streets
again, on parole, after only a few years: many to do it all over again. Mick
has done nothing at all like that but he's the one they have wanted to keep in
prison – downright disgusting. It's all because he's made himself strong and has
retaliated against the inhumane way he's been treated in prison. Over 40 years
kept in solitary confinement; that's one of the reasons he has to wear glasses
because he's been kept in the dark all that time (definitely not even the basic
prison requirement for solitary). He's been taunted by one particular prison governor who didn't like him. This man used to stand outside Mick's cell and taunt
him 'I'll make your time here pure hell'. He even stopped and withheld all Mick's
post and any contact with friends and family. When Mick was eventually moved
elsewhere there were mailbags full of withheld post. It's disgusting all the things
that have gone on over the years. Mick has been treated like a wild animal. If

you continually treat an animal with cruelty and beatings that animal will, over time, turn on his tormentors, as Mick did. He suffered cruel, inhumane treatment. Put yourself in his shoes, what would you do? Of course, none of these treatments ever got reported to the media. The public only ever heard that Mick had kicked off again, never the true reasons behind his behaviour. On one occasion he was told that he could attend his dad's funeral He was all dressed ready and waiting in his cell when a couple of screws said to him 'oh, you're not being allowed to go the funeral now'. What did Mick do on hearing that news? Yes, he retaliated. The consequences were reported in the media but not the reasons behind it. These injustices have happened throughout almost all his captivity. Only last year a prison governor accused Mick of attacking him. They wanted Mick to be tried at the Crown Court so that he would get another 10 – 15 years added onto his sentence. Mick refused to plead guilty – why should he, he didn't do it. This resulted in him appearing in court before a judge and jury of 12 men and women. The screws and governor stood up in court, under oath, and told the judge that Mick had attacked him. Mick was his own Counsel, he didn't have a solicitor to speak on his behalf and the entire jury all came to the same verdict – NOT GUILTY! Result! How good was that! You see the truth is coming out now. The truth, the whole truth and nothing but the truth, so help me God!

Another thing I find annoying is that there is hardly anything reported in the press about all of his charity works. All the proceeds from any of his art sold through auctions, etc. goes to charity. Mick supports so many charities; he helps the homeless, he helps sick children, he donates to Claire House hospice (situated on the site of Clatterbridge hospital where Mike was born). He's donated money to the mother of Keith Bennett, that poor boy whose body has never been found on the moors, killed by Brady and Hindley, when he found out she was running out of funds to find her boy and continue digging for his body. All the good he does through his artwork is rarely reported in the press. It is now time, at long last, for him to go onto the footpath towards freedom and to give him, and his frail mum who is 91, the peace they so deserve. Mick has now been granted an open parole hearing which means members of the public can be present in court and hear the true facts instead of the foregone conclusions that were formerly made behind closed doors, unscrutinised. The truth will out in the end. Actually, when Mick donated his artwork to raise money for the family of Keith Bennett, it was one of the few true things the media ever wrote about him.

Chapter Fourteen: Meeting Frankie Fraser

Ray Williams, the man who got in touch with me wanting to get Mick and Mike in contact with one another again after all those years, became a kind and loyal friend to Mike and I really right up to the time of his death a few years ago. We both went to his funeral to show our respect to his wife and family. Rest in peace Ray.

Most Friday nights my friends and I used to go into Chester for a fun night out. We had our favourite places we used to enjoy going to for a few drinks and a dance. One such place was the Globe. It was down by the canal not far from a great pub we also liked to visit. We'd usually stay at the Globe until the early hours of the morning and on the odd occasion we'd bump into Ray and his friends, Derek and Roger who was Frankie Fraser's manager. He often used to organise charity events on Frankie Fraser's behalf. These men were always very protective of me and my friends. Sometimes we had to watch what we were saying because if we mentioned someone or other was being a nuisance, you could be sure that at least one of them would pick up on it and we'd have to backtrack in case they decided to sort the person out!

After I appeared on one of the documentaries on tv, Ray told me that all the bigtime gangsters in London were delighted that I hadn't gone on tv and slagged Mick off. Last year, in fact, one of them actually said to me that they were so proud of me for defending Mick! Ah, I thought, that was dead nice. Well it was, wasn't it!

Roger used to wing walk for charity, he'd think nothing of standing on a plane when it was airborne. He asked me and my good friend Elaine if we would be interested in doing some wing walking for charity. But oh no, not me! I'm terrified of heights! It would have been my worst nightmare come true and you can guarantee that if I had done it, I would have fallen off the plane and not be here now writing about it! Elaine seemed quite interested in doing it though but something stopped her from taking it any further – probably fear! I remember one of the charity events we attended was at the Slow Boat Chinese restaurant in Chester. Mike came with one of his friends and Elaine came with me and we sat on the table with Ray and Derek, right next to Frankie Fraser and his manager. We were surprised to see seated near Frankie was an ex London police officer who'd been responsible long ago for helping put Frankie behind bars! They seemed the best of friends and often attended charity functions together.

The whole room had loads of tables and at all of them were sat gangsters all in black suits looking very smart but also a bit intimidating. When Frankie Fraser made his speech , he introduced me as Charles Bronson's wife – "Ex-wife!" I shouted out. Oh we were so well looked after that night! We never had an empty glass and the food was delicious. The strange thing about this event was that there were a few of our Friday night (male) friends there too. They were saying to me 'What are you doing here?' and I said to them 'What are you doing here too?'. It was really funny, we were all a bit surprised to see one another there. I'll never forget that night, we were treated like royalty. I also remember being at another charity event when a gentleman was pointed out to me as being a former Met police officer who had also been in the pay of the Krays!

Frankie Fraser was sometimes referred to in his gangster years as Mad Frankie Fraser the dentist. His full name was Francis Davidson and he was an English gangster who also spent a lot of time in prison like Mick. I think he was incarcerated for 42 years roughly, for numerous violent offences. He was part of Britain's underworld between 1940s and 1960s. In 1967 he had an additional 10 year sentence added on as he was implicated along with the notorious Richardson brothers in the Torture Trials. These were the longest trials in British criminal history. They were charged with burning, electrocuting and whipping those found guilty of disloyalty by a kangaroo court. Fraser was nicknamed 'The Dentist' when accused of pulling out the teeth of his victims with pliers During the 1950s, Frankie's main occupation was as a bodyguard to a well known gangster called Billy Hill. He took part in many bank robberies and spent a lot of time in prison and was eventually certified insane and sent to Broadmoor hospital. This is where he met Mick and the two became good friends. Apparently, Frankie was invited to take part in the Great Train Robbery but chose not to as he was already on the run from the police at the time. Frankie knew the Kray twins really well and attended all of the brothers' funerals when they passed on. He also sat with Reggie Kray when he was on his death bed in 2000.

Frankie was also treated unjustly by the prison service, similar to Mick, and this resulted in floggings,beatings and loss of remission. Frankie did come out of prison later on in his life and became a celebrity. He also appeared in a few crime films, such as Hard Men and Lock, Stock and Two Smoking Barrels. He also had a documentary made about his life called The Ultimate Gangster; a DVD which also featured Mick and other notorious gangsters in it. The couple of times I met Frankie Fraser, I always thought he was so polite, funny, well mannered and a charming man. He died in 2014 aged 90 of complications during surgery.

On one of our Friday nights out in Chester, Elaine and I rang for a taxi to take us back to Heswall at the end of the evening whilst the other girls got a separate cab back to their homes in Chester. After we had been in the cab for about 10 minutes, the driver asked us if we knew the men who were in the car behind us. We both looked around and saw 4 men sitting in a Mercedes which appeared to be following us. We didn't recognise them but the driver told us that the car had been following us since we had got into his taxi. He said he had turned off the main road a few times to try and shake them off but they were still following us. He had started to get worried, so he told us he was going to pull up in to the car park of a nearby club and had radioed other taxi drivers to be there to meet us. The next thing we knew we had six taxis in a line following our taxi and they stayed there until we had both arrived home safely. It was very strange, we had no idea who those men were or why they were following us in our taxi. Needless to say, the Mercedes with the four men in turned around at the club car park and we saw no more of them. All very weird, I still wonder what they had planned to do. It all could have been very innocent – or not!!!

Chapter Fifteen: At The Races

Around this time, I noticed that I was feeling more and more psychic. My friends and I used to love to go to Chester Races in May and June. We would all get dressed up and have a ball. We used to all sit in the champagne tent, sometimes I don't think we even got to see any horses! Ah no, only joking, honest I am!

One of the girls was really into the races and which horses to bet on. She used to get tips from horsey friends and was always looking at their form in the racing papers, whereas Elaine and I just picked out names that we liked, regardless of the odds. We would share a bet between us, usually no more than a fiver, and if we ever did win, we would only get about £2.50 each back, but never mind! I was also going through a phase of knowing which horses would not be number 1 and win, but come in second or third. This lasted for a few race meeting and our serious betting friend used to go out and bet large amounts of money on horses which had good odds. I used to tell her 'that horse is not going to win' but she always ignored my advice and, yes, they usually came in second or third, like I predicted.

One of these times, a man who was putting a bet on asked my advice on which horse was going to win. I told him the two horses that he favoured wouldn't win but come in second. He too ignored my advice and went ahead and placed money on each of them to win. Exactly as I predicted they didn't win but came in second. God, the man went mad! I said to him 'I told you they wouldn't win'. It was a really strange phase of my life.

I also met a millionaire at Chester Races one summer. He was from just outside Essex and was married but his wife was an invalid who had a live-in nurse to look after her. I can't even remember his name now but he wasn't my usual type, I preferred taller men. He was about my age but he was also about my size! The afternoon of the races was lovely and then later on in the evening he took my friend and I to the bar at the Grosvenor Hotel and bought us bottles of Moet, I think we drank about 3 bottles between us. It got very late and he booked taxis for us and paid the driver in advance. The following day he rang me and asked if he could take me out for dinner that evening whilst he was staying at the Grosvenor. I declined, as I had been in work all day and couldn't be bothered getting ready to go out again when I got home. We made a date to go to the races again one Friday afternoon meeting. He picked me up from home in a fabulous Bentley sports car and off we went to the races. Everything promised to be a lovely day. He asked which champagne I preferred and ordered a bottle for me. The weather was glorious and I settled down to a wonderful day. He started to study the race programme and told me he was just going to put a couple of bets on and asked if I wanted to go with him. I said no as we'd lose our table and was quite happy sipping my champagne in the sun. Oh happy days! Oh, I forgot to mention that I picked a horse out too and gave the millionaire a fiver to put a bet on for me. Take note of this bit! He took the fiver off me and went off to place our bets. He soon came back to our table and we watched the race together. My horse didn't win and I lost my fiver but he won about five thousand pounds! I'm not joking he'd won all that money and was a millionaire as well. I'll admit I was a bit miffed as he'd obviously been given a good tip and he hadn't shared it with me. He asked me to go with him to collect his winnings which the bookie had kept in a safe for him. I've no idea why he wanted me to go with him but off we went, collected the winnings then went back to our table and drank more champagne. My God I wondered, is he going to share his winnings with me – even my fiver back would have been gratefully received. But no, he didn't give me a penny of it and it put me right off him big time. What a tight man, he takes me out for the afternoon to the races, he doesn't pay for my bet and after winning all that money doesn't give me a penny of it. I definitely wasn't happy with him at all, but I was very good I stayed with him all afternoon and we had some food at the Grosvenor later and loads more Moet. The music was playing and it was getting dead busy in there and whilst I was sitting with the mean millionaire, a bloke I knew from our Friday nights out came over and started chatting. Soon we were dancing together and I never went back to the mean millionaire at all. God, I hate tight men and I'm not sorry to say that I never spoke to the millionaire again.

On another races day out later on in the year, I found I couldn't put my foot down on the floor in one of the pubs we visited in the evening. Unknown to me and my friends I had actually broken my ankle. No-one noticed or knew what had happened; all we could remember was that a doorman had to help me down the stairs when we left. We had no idea at all but, to be honest, we had all had a lot to drink and that was probably the reason I didn't feel any pain and found it quite easy to walk on my heel. The following day I noticed my ankle had started to swell and was turning purple but I still had no idea what I'd done to it. My son, JD, took one look at it and said that he would take me to A & E to get it checked out. When the doctor looked at it he told me I'd broken my ankle and chipped my heel – I was shocked I certainly wasn't expecting that. He set my leg in plaster right up to my knee and asked if I needed any pain-killers which I refused as I think I was still anaethetised by the alcohol from the night before. Then he gave me two crutches - oh God, how I hated those flipping crutches – I just couldn't get the hang of them. You see I'm terrified of heights and having to lift one foot off the floor to balance and walk was dead difficult and if I had to go up a kerb, even a small one, made me really scared. I preferred to get down on my behind and pull myself onto the step or kerb.

My bedroom at that time was up loads of stairs which sort of went into a bend half way up and because it was an old house they were a bit difficult to negotiate. You could never walk too quickly down them, I remember JD one day coming down those stairs into the kitchen and he fell and ended up sliding down the stairs and into the cat's litter tray - it went everywhere. Anyway, I soon found a way to manoeuvre the stairs. I used to put a Tesco carrier bag around my neck and go down on my bottom. Anything I needed to carry I put in the bag. Problem solved! Well one, anyway.

I used to make a cup of tea in the kitchen, making my way by holding onto the sink, then the table , slide my foot along then hold on to something else. Now the only problem I then had was how to get my cup of tea into the lounge. 'I know' I thought I'd had a brainwave 'I'll slide my tea along the table to the end , then I'll put it onto a kitchen chair, then slide the chair with the tea on it into the lounge bit by bit. This worked really well, the only down side was that there was hardly any tea left in my cup when I finally got to sit down in the lounge to drink it! Oh well, never mind hey, but how I hated those crutches, really, really hated them. I'm just so relieved at this moment in time that no-one was killed!

Around this time, one of the almost daily newspaper articles about Mick said he was going to open a restaurant in London when he was released, called Broncos. Mike was going to be one of the chefs and all the waitresses and waiters were going to wear prison screws uniforms and carry large bunches of keys around their waists which jangled when they moved. The meals were all going to be named after all the prisons Mick had been in, such as Wakefield fish and chips, Walton sausage and mash etc. He had even written a menu with all the prices on it but the prices were the same as when he had first entered the prison system. The reporter writing the article said that Mick would be bankrupt within six months of opening if he charged those prices. This was a t a time when Mick was waiting for his parole hearing and I personally am dead sure that if Mick had been released and Mike had been the chef it would have been a great success. Sadly though, Mick never came out, his parole was again refused and all their plans were in vain. Another broken dream for Mick and Mike.

Thinking about this time I remember in a book Mick had written in which he tells the story of something the prisoners used to do to get back at the screws. When the prisoners had sweets, particularly sweets with wrappers on them, they would take the wrappers off and push them inside their behinds then take them out and rewrap them! They would then offer these to the screws. I guess they got the same sort of satisfaction as I got with my stress relief practices.

Chapter Sixteen: Just Like Heaven

By this time my lovely mum had died and God do I miss her, God bless her soul. I still put her favourite pale blue nightie under my pillow every night, it's starting to smell a bit dusty now but I'm too scared to wash it in case I wash off her smell. I find it very comforting. I also used to wear my mum's slippers which were too big for me and over time my big toes started to rub the toes of them away and popped out until the day I was making gravy and dropped a whole pan of it all over my feet and mum's slippers. They couldn't be saved so I had to throw them away which is probably just as well actually as they caused me to trip on many occasions and, once or twice, caused me to trip going down the stairs and I had to stop myself from breaking my neck. Ah, my sweet mum, I do miss her.

One morning on my way to work on the bus I was thinking about her and as I looked out of the window and looked up into the sky and was thinking to myself 'How high are you mum, in heaven?' That night I had an amazing dream about actually going to heaven. Reading this you'll probably be thinking 'What?! She's a nutter!' But I honestly think it was true. What happened in the dream was I was in the sky just floating – just high enough to be able to see below me. It was like looking down from an aeroplane after take-off, you can still make out winding roads and buildings. Then the next moment I was standing quite high up , almost as if I was on a high balcony or similar, looking all around me at the most beautiful scenes of the sea and waves crashing against the shores of little islands. I was talking to someone but have no idea who it was and was shouting out 'It's so beautiful! How beautiful! '. I looked all around me and asked 'Where am I? I'm not on holiday anywhere, I don't recognise this place'. Then I realised I was in heaven. I said to myself I must have died. But, do you know what? I felt the most peaceful I have ever felt in my life. I didn't panic or think 'oh no, what about my family' as I would normally have done.

I then found myself walking in Liverpool One towards Ann Summers where I work but everyone walking towards me just walked straight through me, even though I could see them, they obviously couldn't see me at all. I then found myself in work in the little staff room and dear Maria was sitting down at the table eating her lunch. I picked her lunch up from the table right in front of her and really freaked her out as she couldn't see me. Now Maria and I often play tricks on one another – we jump out on one another or hide from each other but this time it was all real. Sweet little Maria nearly always managed to make me jump with fright , which at my age nearly always results in my wetting myself, or worse still, farting. The thing is I can never, ever get her back although it's not through lack of trying. Oh I do love little Maria, my little work angel!

The next thing I remember was I was walking around the stockroom wearing a purple lacy eye mask from our bondage department. All the girls in turn saw this eye mask moving around but they couldn't see me, which again freaked them all out. I then remember standing behind a woman I didn't know and all the girls were standing together in a group in front of us. I have no recollection of what she was saying to them, but I think she was a medium who the girls had invited in to try and find out what was happening in the shop. I do remember standing by her shoulder saying 'Tell them it's me, it's Irene!'

I don't remember any more after this. Did I visit heaven? I definitely believe I did but what do you think? Anyway, up until my heavenly experience we have not had any purple lacy masks in our bondage department. If we ever do I'll know that my time in this life is nearly over and I had better get all my goodbyes done!. Mmmmm.

Not long after my heavenly experiences, it was actually little Maria who had a weird experience whilst in work. Bear in mind now that she was a sceptic, she certainly didn't believe in ghosts. But one morning she went into work early to start merchandising the big delivery we had received the day before. She was working in the delivery room which has a massive mirror at one end and she was busy working away facing this mirror when suddenly she saw the reflection of a woman with long black hair, dressed all in black, walking across the room. No, it wasn't me! The woman just disappeared into the corridor. Weird hey! But sweet little Maria didn't freak out too much and carried on with the delivery. She is now a believer! God bless her.

Another time I had an unusual experience which felt as if I was back in time in the olden days, 19th century, I think. Again, I was talking to someone but couldn't see who it was. I remember looking at all the old houses in a little street when a penny farthing bike went past us and one of the very first cars went along the street in front of us. All the time I could hear gunfire in the background, which I think were muskets. That was another very strange experience! I'm just being clever now by telling you about the penny farthings! It was designed by a British Victorian, James Starkey, and was the first bike. Its name comes from the large front wheel and small back wheel which resembled the largest and smallest coins of that time. The larger the front wheel the further you can travel on one rotation of the pedals. They were very popular in the late 19th century and normally purchased by rich men. The wheels were solid rubber and so you never got a puncture; I am so very happy that we have bicycles that are so much easier to ride nowadays as most of you probably know I am a bike person (I can't pass my driving test!). Just imagine me going downhill on a penny farthing! Apparently, you had to put your legs over the handle bars, no that's definitely not me. Thank God!

There is life after death. You do go to a better place. I have actually seen my beloved grandson who passed whilst he was a baby. His name is Jayki and he came to visit me one morning when I was sitting up in bed. I'd just plumped up my pillows to get into a comfortable position to read. As I tuned around I jumped – there was Jayki standing by my side right by my bed. I jumped because I wasn't expecting anyone to be there, and as I jumped he giggled - it was absolutely lovely! But then, sadly, he disappeared. I can remember

Never ride a bike without a saddle: Charlie Salvador

every detail about him, his clothes, his face, his beautiful black wavy hair, lovely olive skin and the most beautiful big, dark eyes. He was actually the age he would have been had he grown up in this world. I can't explain how wonderful it was to see him and to hear him giggle because he had made me jump. Ah, I know that I was truly blessed to have been given this remarkable experience. Thank you God!

'Your hopes and your futures are all rooted in heaven, where eternal ecstasy awaits you. You have an eternity of problem-free living reserved for you in heaven. Rejoice in that inheritance which no one can take it away from you. At the end of your life path is the entrance to heaven. Ask and it will be given to you, knock and the door will be open to you.'

This I truly believe with all my heart.I have put this paragraph into my book be-cause it comes from a lovely book called 'Jesus Calling' by Sarah Young. I was given this book by a close friend and found it to be very helpful and true. It helps you become much more positive and less anxious. I actually go to bed with it by my side and hold it whilst I sleep - it's so comforting, like a hot water bottle on your stomach. I would definitely recommend you buy it, it's so positive. 'Your hope and your future are rooted in Heaven where eternal ecstasy awaits you!'

As time went on Mick, was becoming more and more infamous. He had become a con celebrity as he was often referred to by the media. Some of the newspaper articles were so disturbing and shocking to Mike and myself. Were they true? One article about the time Mick kidnapped the art teacher shows Mick as being mad. This was at a time in his life when Mick was at his worst; he had nothing left to live for. He had lost his nan, dad and older broth-er and was not allowed to attend any of their funerals although he had been promised by prison authorities that he could attend. He was being inhumanely treated in prison, had constant harassment, frequently beaten by the heavy mob and treated like a wild animal with any hope he had of ever getting out taken away from him. Where is the logic in the fact that if another prisoner commits crimes but if Mick attacks that prisoner in self defence it's Mick who gets more time added to his sentence. As Mick says, if you land one punch in prison you get 20 back at you.

With the Iraqi hijackers, Mick was let out of his cell (was it accidentally on purpose? this does happen a lot in prison) and he ended up getting twice as much time added to his sentence than the Iraqis who had hijacked a plane full of women and children. It makes no sense at all. He took 11 of these Iraqis hostage 3 times in one day – how was he able to do that?

It was a very black time for us all. This went on for years and years, over 44 years in fact and, yes, they did have a big impact on our lives, especial-ly Mike's. We both have a very vivid imagination – you just have to focus on one day at a time. It's been absolutely horrendous for both of us. This is all depicted in one of Mick's latest pieces of art. It shows Mick and I at the very beginning, then it shows the madness, that all went on from his treatment. He's even well known and popular in many other countries. In Thailand when a family member was working there, she mentioned one of the bars had a full size poster of Mick on the wall. I would even go so far as to say that his reputation has spread worldwide, don't you think?

I have terrible nightmares on a regular basis, some horrendous and really frightening. They all seem to have a gangster theme. Sometimes it's me holding a machine gun in the middle of a circle shooting everyone dead, other times it's someone else doing the shooting. I don't know them but in my nightmares they are all gangsters. Sometimes, gangs of them are chasing me and I'm desperately trying to find hiding places to get away from them; other times I'm climbing up high stone walls trying to escape. It's always a big relief when I wake up, thank God.

I'm afraid Mike has not been able to handle it all too well. He chose to do other things to help him try and forget the past. Twenty-five years ago Mike was wrongly accused of being involved in a drug related crime and was held in remand in Walton prison for 3 months. I know everyone in prison always says they are innocent but Mike was innocent and eventually the case was dropped , but the three months spent there was a terrifying time for Mike and also brought back echoes of Mick's time there for me. I couldn't believe this was happening to me again. I couldn't face it and it made me ill. I kept thinking if any of the inmates there knew he was Mick's son, they may try and beat him up and boast that they had beaten up Bronson's boy. It was a very bad time and I was close to having a breakdown. You only have to look at Mike and you'll know who his dad is, they are so alike. When Mick appeared on tv doing one of his roof protests you could see him quite clearly and everyone said at the time 'isn't Mike like his dad'. I even thought it was Mike when I first saw it, my heart was beating so fast I thought I was going to have a heart attack. When Mike walks into any venue, such as pubs and clubs, you hear people saying 'Oh look Bronson's in the room', or something to that effect.

Mick didn't know any of this at the time – in fact, I don't think he knows about it at all. A big worry for me at the time was that they would keep Mike in prison for ever just like they had his dad if the authorities knew who his dad was. Oh, I can't describe how vulnerable and scared and nervous I was. Horrible, horrible times.

One of these times Mike was supposed to have attended court and would have been able to come home. I attended and the prison authorities had forgotten he was supposed to attend so I came home from court without Mike. I got home, walked into my bedroom and just screamed and screamed. I couldn't seem to stop and knew I was close to losing it altogether. There seemed to be a voice inside my head telling me to scream louder and louder but I knew I had to fight these voices in order to survive and help Mike. My family made sure I wasn't left on my own for a couple of weeks after that. I suppose you could say I'm a survivor. Everyone says how strong I am but sometimes though, in fact a lot of times, I certainly don't feel strong. I just want to feel happy and at peace.

Because Mike was on remand, he was allowed to have a few visits a week. I'll never forget the first time we went to visit him. Leicia (Mike's half sister), my mum and myself went through into the visitors room and when we got to see him we all got very upset. He looked terrible and asked us to get him out of there. That's a heart breaking thing to cope with – I'm his mum but I couldn't do anything to help him. Another nightmare time for us to live through. I do know though that I wouldn't be here today if it wasn't for my mum. She came with me every single time and was so supportive. This was all new to mum. She was a gentle lady, she had never seen a family member in those circumstances but she took that journey into horror with me to give me the strength to carry on. We used to get the bus to Liverpool city centre and then we'd get a taxi to Walton prison. Quite often the taxi drivers were really funny and would try to make us laugh to cheer us up on our journey. I remember one taxi driver said to mum 'Is it your fella who's inside, luv?' Mum was completely horrified that he should think that! 'It is certainly not' she said in a posh voice. Ah, bless you mum! We did laugh then about it. Mum went on to tell him that we came form Neston on the Wirral. The taxi driver didn't know where it was so mum told him it was near Parkgate where all the shrimps come from. This made him and I laugh, my laughter probably more from nerves though.

When we used to go to visit Mike, we were shown into a waiting room to wait along with the other visitors. We were each given our own key and locker to put our handbags in. On one particular visit mum was holding a large umbrella which was too big for the locker, so mum decided to just leave it on a chair until we get back. A prison officer overheard her and said to her 'you can't leave anything on a chair here, love, this is a prison it's full of thieves, it'll be gone before you get back!' We laughed about it later, you had to be there to see the funny side.

Mum was quite a funny person but she didn't realise just how funny she was as she could sometimes be a little haughty. I remember sometimes on a Sunday mum and I used to go out into Neston for our Sunday lunch and mum would love a Baileys or three. We'd go to a big, newish pub for our lunch which has since closed down; one of about six in Neston. She knew that one of her younger brothers, Uncle George, liked to go out for a few drinks on a Sunday lunchtime. If we didn't see him when we were having our lunch, she insisted in looking in the other local pubs to see if we could spot him. Off we would go, if there was no sign of him, mum would go up to any stranger and say 'Has our George been here today?' as if everyone knew which George she was talking about and if they said 'George who?' she would get really annoyed. 'Our George' she would say. God bless you mum!

At one of these Sunday lunches, mum would sometimes take her false teeth out. She had 3 side teeth on a plate which she said she couldn't eat properly with. So she took them out and wrapped them in a serviette until she'd finished eating. This day there was no sign of 'our George' so we left the pub to walk back home. Once we'd walked for about 35 minutes, she suddenly remembered she had left her false teeth in the serviette on the table in the restaurant. I phoned the restaurant up and they said they'd look for them and ring us back. They did phone us back and said that the waiter had cleared our table and thrown our used serviettes into the rubbish bin. Ah, do you know what? The poor man emptied all the rubbish out of the bin and rooted around in it until he found mum's teeth. Wasn't that kind of him! I walked back to the pub to get mum's teeth and gave the waiter £20 which mum had given me to give to him as a thank-you. Poor bloke though, what a horrible thing he had to do.

Chapter Seventeen: Paula

A lot of the media at this time was all about Mick getting married to a woman called Paula Williamson. She eventually became his third wife. The romance started when she began writing to Mick in prison and they became good friends which developed into a romantic relationship. Mike and I weren't told anything about this in the beginning – we only knew what we had read in the papers about her. I was in work one day when a presenter from This Morning rang me asking if they could talk to me. Apparently, they had tried to contact me via Facebook wanting to appear on the show to talk about Mick and Paula's upcoming wedding. This was quite a shock to Mike and myself as it was just out of the blue. Mike was upset, especially when it was reported that the wedding would only be attended by close family members. Now what is a 'close family member'? I would say that Mike being Mick's only child, would be classed as such, wouldn't you? Personally, I thought it was just another time when Mike was overlooked by Mick.

Anyway, This Morning, offered to pay for my return train ticket to London and a fee of £1,200 to appear on the show. They wanted me to go down to London the following night. 'Oh, no' I thought to myself 'there's no way I'm going to appear on TV in the morning without having my hair done and sorting out what I am going to wear'. It was decided then that I should go down a day later and appear on the Friday morning show with Eamonn and Ruth hosting it instead of Holly and Phil if I'd gone on the earlier show. The following day I had time to get my hair done and sorted out which dress I was going to wear and even practised sitting on a chair to see which look would look best to my advantage on tv. I think it was my legs which were shown to their advantage judging by all the comments from both male and female viewers I received – oh, and my pale pink, soft leather ankle boots!

When I had got myself ready, I packed an overnight bag to take to London with me and then left by taxi to Liverpool Lime Street station to get the train down. The journey there, well all I can say is that it would have made a funny 'Carry On' film. The first obstacle I had was getting my pre-paid tickets. I walked to a big office on the station and through the glass I could see a couple of women sitting at their desks. 'Oh' I said to myself 'this must be where I have to go to get them' but the problem was I couldn't get the glass doors to open. The two women were shouting instructions to me but I still had no idea how to get those doors open. Then a lovely old lady appeared who was struggling with two large suitcases and a big bag and she opened the door for me. God bless her. Then one of the women told me I needed to get the ticket from the machine on the platform. My mind was in turmoil. 'Which machine does she mean, how do you get the ticket out of it and how do I open these damn doors again to get out? 'This time a kind gentleman saw me struggling and held the doors open for me. Thank God! Now all I had to do was get the tickets out of the machine. Anyone who knows me and machines or anything electronic, even simple tasks, sometimes take me ages to figure them out. I didn't like the machine at all. You had to put a number in then your credit card, even though they were pre-paid. What a to-do! I had to ask three different people to try and do it for me in the end, I just couldn't follow the instructions at all. With the ticket in my hand I toddled off to use the toilet before I got on the train. 'This shouldn't be too hard' I told myself but you needed the right change to enter the toilets. Then on my third try to get past the barrier, the bloody thing got stuck and wouldn't let me into the cubicle. One of the assistants had to come in and fix it so I could use the loo. Mission accomplished, phew! I didn't want to have to use the toilet on the train. Ugggh.

My next obstacle was finding the right station for my train to Euston. Surprisingly enough, I found it after asking a couple of guards and made my way to my reserved seat on the train. It wasn't first class, but hey! Now, I've got a thing about germs, a really bad fear of catching them. I've always tied something round my mouth on the bus, even pre-Covid, but as soon as I settled down on my seat I realised I didn't have a scarf with me. 'Oh well, it doesn't matter' I thought, 'I've got my anti-bacterial hand gel and anti-bacterial wipes with me, I'll be fine'. So I put my bag on the free seat next to me so no-one else would sit there. A lady came and sat opposite me on the other side of the train and I thought 'that's ok, she's not that close to me'. But of course, it wasn't – she had a cough and instead of sitting straight in her seat she sat at an angle with her legs in the aisle, which meant I was the first stop for all her cough germs. I plastered the anti-bac all over my mouth, nose and hands and kept giving her daggers every time she coughed. After a time I think she got the message as she sat in her seat properly so her germs weren't dead in my pathway.

When we arrived at Manchester, a lot more people got on the train. There are plenty of carriages I thought, please don't come and sit in mine. Another lovely human being got on and sat directly behind me. I didn't worry at this point because the backs of the seats are quite high and if he coughed or sneezed I'd have a bit of cover. Then, ten minutes into our journey, this bloody man started sneezing, not once or twice but about ten times. Out comes my anti-bac again, wipes, gel all over my mouth, nose and hands. Then the coughing started. 'What the hell is wrong with him' I thought. I gave him one of my 'if looks could kill' looks a few times and kept sliding further down my seat to the point that I was nearly on the floor. Anything to escape his germs. In the end I gave up and thought to myself I may as well drink my 2 little bottles of wine I'd bought. If I get a bad cough and cold it's too bad, I may as well just give in. I drank both the bottles and oddly enough it didn't bother me anymore!

The next obstacle was arriving in Euston I had to find the taxi This Morning had arranged to meet me to take me to my hotel. When I got off the train, I had a choice of two exits – which one would the taxi be waiting for me at? Obviously, I took the wrong exit, so when I left the station I couldn't see any taxis at all, just lots of people walking around. My phone kept ringing and when

I answered it the taxi driver directed me to where he was waiting. 'I can't see you' I kept saying .'I'm here, I'm here' he would reply. Now the taxi driver was a lovely man but, because he had a foreign accent, I couldn't understand a word he was saying. Then I saw a lovely, young policeman. I ran up to him almost in tears telling him I couldn't find the taxi driver who was waiting for me. The policeman then took the phone off me and spoke to the driver and then walked me around to the waiting taxi. Had I taken the other exit I wouldn't have got lost at all! Never mind, I have never had a good sense of direction.

The taxi driver dropped me off at my hotel and then all I had to do was check in and settle into my room. I was given my room key and a porter carried my bag and took me up on the lift to my room. The lift gave me an eerie feeling, I hate lifts and try to avoid using them but I told myself I would use the stairs when I'm on my own. I tried to open the door to my room but it just would not open. I tried ten times with no luck so I had to run after the porter and ask him for help to open my door. He had walked along the corridor and was just about to get back in the lift but very kindly came to my assistance. He patiently explained that I was putting the key card into a vent and not where it should go! I thanked him and off he went again and the door opened up into a lovely room with a double bed, a bar, fab bathroom and shower and toilet and also a little sitting room. Now that's what I call a hotel room, just wish I could remember the name of it. Then I decided I would put the lights on, easy peasy I thought. But no, it wasn't a normal light switch but you had to be good at electronics to figure it out. There were all different settings for the lights. Mood lights, bright lights, reading lights – all connected to this computer on the wall. 'Oh dear' I thought I'm going to have to go back downstairs and get someone to come up and put the lights on for me. The same nice porter came back up with me and, whilst he was sorting the lights ou,t I asked him to switch the tv on too. This was high tec also and I never did manage to get it on the channel I wanted. I had to stick with the one channel it was on originally. By this time, I was in need of a strong cup of tea. I looked around the room but could see no sign of the usual tray with cups and kettle and teabags, etc. on. I couldn't see this anywhere so off I go again downstairs to find the poor old porter and asked him if he could find me a kettle. Again, he got back into the lift with me, came into the room, slid open a cupboard and there on a beautiful tray was my kettle and crockery. I did feel a bit silly but hey, never mind. I really regret not given this man a tip when I left, the number of times he had had to come up and down to my room. He must have thought I was a tight so and so but I forgot all about it until I was on my way home.

The next morning, I didn't go down for any breakfast, I stayed in my room and had a coffee and one of my breakfast biscuits. I had a lovely shower, put on my make-up and got dressed and made my way downstairs to the foyer where I was being collected at 9.30am. PS I also had drunk half a small bottle of wine in my room just before I left! I was starting to feel very nervous and needed something to calm my nerves.

The taxi arrived and took me to the ITV studios, just a short distance from my hotel as it turns out. I had to go through a little security check and then wait for one of the team members to come and get me. Now the part of the building I was waiting in was not what you'd expect. It looked like a storage room with old electronic equipment in it. 'What on earth am I doing here' I thought, it was so scruffy. Then a lady came and took me up a couple of flights of stairs to the top part of the building where the studio was. I can't say it was very glamorous, it certainly wasn't as posh as I was expecting. I was shown into the green room furnished with a settee and some armchairs and a large tv on which they showed the recorded shows that appeared live. There were big photos of all the producers on the wall. A kind lady brought me numerous cups of tea but there was no-one else sitting in there to keep me company.

Every now and then someone would walk past the door, regular faces on ITV, then Eamonn walked past a couple of times to his dressing room. He must have come up the back way as well; he smiled at me a few times but didn't come right into the room where I was waiting. Ruth walked past too a few times, then I was called into hair and make-up and a lovely make-up artist did my make-up just like I do it myself. I was so worried at first in case I got someone like they had on the Trisha show but I needn't have worried at all. After a quick chat with a producer, I was shown into a dressing room so that I could get changed. It was an okay room but nothing special. After about fifteen minutes, another team member knocked on my dressing room door and asked if I was ready because they wanted to use the dressing room I was in for Louis Walsh and Shane Richie. As I came out of the room there was Louis and Shane! We all smiled at each other and Louis looked me up and down but in a nice way, an admiring way then I was led back into the green room ready to go on air. After a few minutes Louis came up to me in the green room . He's so lovely, more handsome in real life than tv, and he asked me if I knew where the hair and make-up room was. I showed him the way – it was only a few yards away from us. He thanked me and gave me another admiring look. I was then taken on to the studio floor.

Eamonn came up to me and said 'Ruth, this is Irene'. Ruth then came up to me as well. Eamonn said 'You look lovely' to me, which was nice as it put me at ease. Then I was asked to sit down on the settee ready for the interview to begin. Just before it went on air the producer said to me because of the tight timetable they had to work by, if Eamonn or Ruth asked me something or mentioned an incorrect date, I wasn't to correct them but to leave it at that as the producers would be talking to them through their ear pieces to push on with the interview. They were both lovely even though Eamonn pushed me to speak quickly. By the time I'd thought of the answer Eamonn kept going onto the next question which really didn't help me as I kept forgetting what it was I was going to say. Whatever I said, I had no intention of slagging either Mick or Paula off, if that is what they wanted to hear. It became obvious to me during the interview that Eamonn really had no idea about Mick. He thought everything he had read about Mick in the media was true and that Mick was mad, violent, etc. It was so obvious in his remarks to me but I think I got my own back towards the end of the interview when I asked Eamonn what he would be like if he had spent the last 44 years in solitary confinement. He replied 'Point taken'!. The interview ended and they'd run out of time. Ruth asked me if I was going to stay for the rest of the show because she wanted to know more about Mike but I declined. I wish I had stayed now but at the time all I wanted to do was get myself back home and relax on the journey back. Who knows? Louis may have invited me out to lunch? Mmm, I wonder !!

Much later on, I was told that someone had been told that This Morning had been expecting me to go on and slag Paula and Mick off but I'm afraid they didn't get what they wanted as it's not something I would ever do. It's not in my nature to be nasty like that. The same with this book – if any readers are expecting me to slag Mick off or anyone else in my life, you will be disappointed. I am writing this book as it happened, there are no lies, no nastiness, this story is THE WHOLE TRUTH AND NOTHING BUT THE TRUTH SO HELP ME GOD. Now where did I get this saying from?!

Shortly after my This Morning interview I received a phone call from someone called George Bamby. He said that he had something important to tell me about Mick which also involved Mike. What he went on to tell me shocked me greatly. I suddenly went into shock mode and starting shaking violently. 'Is it true, is it really true?' I asked myself. He told me that he was Mick's illegitimate son and that he wanted to speak to Mike and tell him that he was Mike's half brother. He asked if he could meet up with me and Mike and also bring Paula along, Mick's new wife. At this point in Mike's life I was really worried about the impact this may have on him; I didn't think Mike was in the right frame of mind to be given this information. I told George Bamby I didn't think it was such a good idea at this moment in time but George rang Mike anyway and left a voicemail on Mike's phone to ring him back as he had important news from his dad.

After about an hour I had another call from George Bamby to say that he had spoken to Mike and they had had a lovely, sad conversation in which they were both crying. 'Thank God for that' I said to Bamby. I was so worried about how Mike would take the news. They then made arrangements to meet up with Mike and his then girlfriend in Chester the following day. He said they were a lovely couple and not to worry when I went to meet Paula and Bamby myself at the weekend. In fact, when Mike met Bamby he told Mike to say that they had each had a DNA test done to prove they were brothers, which was not true. Bamby also asked me to say the same to the press if they rang me, which gave me a slightly uneasy feeling about the whole thing.

Nevertheless, I went to Chester that weekend to meet up with Paula and Bamby and it felt so right. They were a lovely couple. Paula, I felt a certain kinship with straightaway and I liked Bamby too but on closer inspection I must say I couldn't see any resemblance between Bamby and Mike or Mick. Mike is dark like his dad and there is no doubt who his dad is, but Bamby is a lot fairer. When I pointed this out to him he said that his mother was blonde (in fact she looked just like Myra Hindley, he said) whilst I was very dark and that was why there was no resemblance between them. Anyway, this gave me another little twinge of doubt.

My granddaughter actually looked George Bamby up on the internet at that time and she told me to be very careful because Bamby impersonates other people to obtain stories for the papers, etc. Another thing to make me doubtful. When I went into work before the meeting with them in Chester, my mind was all over the place. Did Mick do the dirty on me? Was Bamby's mum pregnant the same time as I was. I kept dropping things all that day in work because I couldn't seem to concentrate.' Is it true, isn't it?' If it's not true then why pretend? He even went to meet Mick's elderly mum as her long lost grandson. If that wasn't the case, then why say it?

Bamby told me that his mum had been very cruel to him and had abused him as a child. She had also set fire to him as part of that abuse. All in all, he had had a terrible life up to the point when another family had fostered him. My thoughts at the time were that if he really was Mick's son, we should have taken him in and brought him up with Mike when he was a baby. I hated the idea that he had been abused, I felt so sorry for him.

Then I remembered the time that two women came to our house in Little Sutton many years ago looking for Mick. One of them was heavily pregnant – was it with Mick's child? – I don't know but if so it would have meant that Bamby was 6 months younger than Mike when in fact he's six months older than him. More doubt set in. Bamby has been asked many times by Mike and also by Mark, Mick's younger brother, to do a DNA test but he always refuses to do so. In time the truth will out, I'm sure.

George Bamby appeared on tv on This Morning to tell the viewers he was Mick's long lost son. As he spoke, there were a lot of things that didn't add up or make sense to me. For example, he said he had knocked on Mick's door in Little Sutton to tell him in person that he was his son. That didn't make any sense to me as Mick hadn't lived at that house since he first went to prison when Bamby was a toddler. Little points like that he made which didn't ring true and weren't quite right. The only thing that will solve the mystery is to have a DNA test done. Mike and his Uncle Mark had hoped this would happen but so far, despite numerous requests, it still hasn't happened. Mike and I doubt he is who he says he is. So, that's that!

Some years later, Paula got in touch with me again to ask if I would like to appear with her on Loose Women. The programme was about exs being friends. Usually exs don't get on well but Paula and I did. We were so very alike in so many ways, we always laughed and laughed together about the same sort of things. The programme makers wanted us to show the viewers just how well we got along together. It was being filmed at Easter so therefore there would be a lot of school children watching it as well in their school holidays and the producers asked us to make the interview light and fun, which I think we certainly did!

The night before, Paula travelled down to London and I travelled down by train from Liverpool. Loose women had booked us into the Mondrian Hotel just a few short steps from the ITV studios and was also Paula's favourite hotel. Paula arrived first and she messaged me as soon as she arrived. I must say the hotel was out of this world! I had thought the hotel I stayed in when I was on This Morning was posh but The Mondrian was double, double posh, honestly! My room looked out directly onto the river. Sightseers on river cruises would go past and wave to me standing on my terrace! It was magical. I could see all the sights from my room – St Pauls cathedral, the Eye, the Shard, Tower Bridge, everything! I loved it so much, I was so excited then Paula came into my room and we just held on to one another and jumped up and down like little school children. Out we went for a drink to a nearby pub for a few Proseccos. I had told Paula I didn't want a late night or to get too drunk because I wouldn't be able to handle going into the studios the following day with a hangover. Anyway, we sat in the bar and almost drunk the whole bottle of Prosecco between us. Paula suddenly said 'I've just realised, we asked for a bottle of sweet Prosecco and this is dry'. So the waiter brought us another bottle of sweet Prosecco that we didn't have to pay for. We drank the entire bottle and noticed that the pub had emptied out and we were the only customers there. The waiters had started putting the chairs under the tables and generally tidying up the place. Ah, bless them, they didn't ask us to leave but gave us two plastic beakers to drink the remains of our wine when they took our glasses away to wash them. We did feel mean about keeping the staff there so we took our beakers and left the pub. We stood outside drinking and laughing our heads off saying 'oh my God, we might get arrested for drinking outside' as we were stood right by a sign that forbids drinking outside. ' What if we get arrested before we go on Loose Women' we joked. They will have to tell their viewers that Charles Bronson's wives were in the cells after being arrested. We thought it was hilarious and couldn't stop laughing. The press would have had a field day.

When we eventually got back to our hotel we headed for the roof top bar for a few more drinks – so much for my resolve to not have much to drink. I had a glass of Prosecco and Paula had a couple of cocktails then we went back to my room and ordered room service. We drank more Proseccos sitting on my terrace overlooking the Thames and all the beautiful sights of London at night. It was sheer bliss. Bu this time it was 5.30 am and I said to Paula 'I've got to get to bed now or I'll never wake up in time for our visit to the studios'. She agreed with me and went back to her room after making arrangements to meet in the foyer at 9.30 the following morning.

I awoke after very little sleep and had a shower, put on some of my eye make-up and changed into my little black dress already to go and meet Paula downstairs. There was no sign of Paula so I went and helped myself to some breakfast in the restaurant. Still no sign of her so I rang her and she said she'd be down in 5 minutes. I had a quick look around the hotel, the inside of which was made to look like a luxury ship with portholes – very luxurious and trendy. Once Paula arrived by my side, we checked out and walked just around the corner to the ITV studios. I noticed a long line of mainly women wating to go in and presumed it was the live audience for Loose Women. They all stared at us as we walked past and I wondered if they recognised us. We went to a different entrance to the one I'd been to before – Paula took us to the main entrance and to a receptionist sitting behind this big, long, curved desk. We gave her our names and she told us to wait for the producer to come and get us.

We were collected from the reception area and shown into Hair and Make-up where the Loose Women presenters where also having the hair and make-up done. They were Kaye Adams, Nadia Sawalha, Stacey Soloman and another lady, I can't remember her name. They were all so lovely and immediately put me at ease and made us feel welcome.

From there we were shown into our dressing room where we could have snacks and soft drinks or tea and coffee (definitely no alcohol!). We were then told again by the presenter to keep the interview light and funny as there would be children watching the show at home. We certainly did that alright, as I couldn't stop laughing at times when I looked at Paula. That's how we were when we were together, just giggling all the time like naughty children. Ah God bless Paula, I'll always miss her.

Just before we went on, we were taken into the Green Room and had some photographs taken. Then a pop star came in and sat with us until it was his time to go on. He was really lovely and we all got on very well together. I can't remember his name at this moment in time but I'm sure it'll come to me. When the time came for us to go on and be interviewed, do you know what? I wasn't at all fazed by all the faces staring at us from the audience. I didn't find it at all scary, I just felt really calm. God know where that came from but I fully enjoyed the whole experience.

Some of the panel tried to make out Mick was this big, bad, mad man and that was the reason he had been kept in prison for so long but they didn't know the real Mick like I did, they only knew what they had read in the papers and seen on the media. It wasn't their fault but I did make the point that if he ever did come out he would be invited on all the chat shows and reality tv and maybe even go on 'I'm a celebrity – get me out of here'. This lead to quite a few of the papers showing a caption of me, Kaye Adams and Mick in the celebrity jungle. I had to laugh at some of the stories, they were really funny.

After the show finished, we had more photos taken with the presenters and then went outside to our waiting car. When we got out, all we could hear were shouts of 'Irene! Paula! Irene! Paula! from the waiting reporters and taking loads of photos of us. Also, there were lots of fans waiting for us – yes, fans – wanting our autographs and taking photos of us. It was insane. We chatted to a lot of the fans and signed our autographs for them. They were really nice and some of them stuck in my mind. I remember seeing a newspaper article a few days later in which one of the fans said how she had met us both and thought we were both really lovely and had a lot of time for them instead of rushing off. How nice was that of her. We then got into our waiting car and it dropped us off at a pub/restaurant place and Paula said to go upstairs where some women were waiting to interview us, I'm not sure what for but it was something she had mentioned previously and I had agreed to. They took photos of us and inter- viewed us separately and together. I think they intended to make a documentary from it but it never happened.

Once it was over, they ordered a taxi for us and paid the fare to Euston station. Paula was meeting a friend there and staying another night in London so we said our goodbyes there and I got my train back home. Sadly, I think that was the last time I ever saw Paula alive. Bless her.

Well, I'd better stop writing for today. It's nearly time for Coronation Street and by the time I've touched everything in my kitchen 5 times, turned the lights off, then on again, I'll just be in time to watch it. One day I would love to be free of having to do these OCD things. The way my life is still going I don't reckon it'll be anytime soon. Oh well, never mind, that's life, but I'll be back.

Chapter Eighteen: Summer Berries

Years ago, after Mike had been to visit his dad with Ray in his high security prison, they started to keep in touch a lot more frequently, but it was always an on off situation. Whenever Mick wrote to Mike, he would always put a letter in for me.

Also, a lot of Mick's friends got in touch with Mike, some serious gangsters, some ordinary people. One of these was Kate Kray who had married Ronnie Kray in 1989 whilst he was in Broadmoor. The marriage lasted until 1994. She has written many books on the British gangland underworld and she is still a good friend of Mick's. I remember also Ronnie Kray writing to Mike after he had met Mick in Broadmoor. Another was gangster Dave Courtney who lives in 'Camelot Castle' in London, the name his friends have given to his home. Mike went to London and stayed with Dave Courtney for the weekend many years ago. Last year Dave Courtney had a charity day for Mick and Tim PPPPPPP (yes, that's his real name – he had it changed by deed poll!) was going to give a talk about Mick. My daughter and I were planning to go and had arranged for Tim to pick us up in his Bronco Buster, a car he had had specially modified to promote Charles Bronson aka Charles Salvador aka Mick Peterson. It had Charles Salvador, Born Again Artist on the sides, it had flags all over it and Mick's signature on the front. It looked fab, a proper show-stopper I thought. We were both looking forward to travelling down to London in it. Mick had also contacted Dave Courtney to tell him we were going and to make sure we were well looked after. Sadly this didn't happen as the event was cancelled due to Covid19.

Mick had told me that Dave Courtney had a sex cellar in his house with all sorts of bondage equipment and wondered what I thought about it. I think he was surprised to learn that I, unlike most people, wouldn't have turned a hair on my head! When I first started at Ann Summers, 17 or 18 years ago, our bondage section at that time was a lot more ferocious and scary looking than it is now. Nowadays, it's really soft bondage, masks, gags, whips, floggers, cuffs and restraints etc. If a man had come anywhere near me with some of the other early bondage stuff I would have run a mile, that's for sure!

Three years ago Mick told me about an art exhibition at the Flux Museum where they were going to exhibit some of his artwork. A lot of his friends would be attending including Tom Hardy (he played Mick in the film), Rod Harrison, Ivor Batey, Dave Ginnelly and also Mike O'Hagon, the ex-prison officer who resigned because of Mick's treatment in prison. Mick asked if I would like to go and I jumped at the chance. My daughter Leicia wanted to come with me and then my grand daughter decided she wanted to come with us too. As it was her birthday and mine a few days before we decided we'd make a special week-end of it and I rented a lovely suite for two nights at the Mondrian Hotel in London for the three of us. They had already heard how I loved the place and the views across the Thames, it was a five star hotel right in the heart of the city (originally called Sea Containers) and I decided I would treat my family to celebrate our birthdays. I booked a suite with a terrace balcony overlooking the river with a queen double bed for Leicia and I and a studio bed for Phoebe. It was ultra trendy; the decorations were out of this world and Phoebe was in her element. I think she must have been a rich guest on the Titanic in a previous life! It was the same hotel that ITV booked Paula and I in when we were on Loose Women.

We travelled down on a Friday tea-time after work and school. We had 1st class seats on the train and I was expecting it to be just like the first-class seats Ian used to book when we went on train journeys to Scotland and London with a la carte menus, silver waitress service and really very posh indeed. We were very disappointed, as it was more like an ordinary train carriage – the only difference being you could use a waiting room before your journey and have free drinks and snacks. On the return journey we couldn't get any free drinks or snacks as they were extra busy and there was nothing left! Bloody typical, we thought!

The train journey was hilarious. I think I must have been in one of my funny moods as everything I said made Leicia, Phoebe and two other passengers laugh their heads off! When we arrived at Euston Station, we went out of the right exit this time, near the taxi stands and got a taxi to take us the short journey to the hotel. When we walked into the hotel, Leicia and Phoebe were both in awe of their surroundings - they said they felt like film stars. When the porter took us up to our room, there was no trouble with the key, putting the lights and tv on this time: that only happens when I'm on my own wherever I go! Phoebe was walking round filming everything on her phone, oh, she was so excited! We went outside and sat on our terrace overlooking the river and whenever people went past on a boat they always waved to us.

There was a lovely surprise waiting for us in the room. The hotel had provided us with a summer berries cake with our names on it. I had mentioned we were celebrating our birthdays when I made the booking and I was hoping they may do something like that but I thought they may have left a bottle of champagne for us too – but hey, you can't have everything can you?! The only problem was that Phoebe, who is a very fussy eater, hates berries so, of course, the cake was a definite no-no. Anyway, we went down into the restaurant for a meal and the staff were fussing around us, especially Phoebe as her birthday was the day before, and ah, bless them, they had taken to trouble to make her a special dessert with her name written in chocolate on the plate. It looked delicious, good enough to eat, actually!, and it was very big, but it had summer berries all over it. You should have seen Phoebe's face! 'Oh no!' she whispered 'it's got summer berries in it, I can't eat it'. Leicia and I looked at each other and burst out laughing. She kept saying she couldn't eat it and the waiter was hovering around expecting to see a look of delight from Phoebe so we asked him if Phoebe could take the special dessert back to our room to eat it later as she was too full to enjoy it at the moment after her meal. It was getting quite late by then, so we all went to bed after a tour of the hotel and especially the gym which Phoebe and I wanted to use in the morning.

I must have woken up about ten times during the night because my darling daughter Leicia snored her head off. In fact, it was so loud at one point I just started to laugh hysterically. She sat up in bed and accused me of waking her up, she wasn't amused. I didn't get much sleep after that and I was annoyed as we were going to the Flux Museum later in the day and I didn't want to be half asleep there. I wanted to look nice and fresh. Phoebe and I went to the gym for an hour on the treadmills and exercise bikes which was great fun. Then Phoebe and Leicia went into the sauna whilst I started to get ready. When they got back it was all rush for us all to get ready and put our make-up on, etc. I tried to open a bottle of wine before we set out for the venue but had to use a pair of scissors as I couldn't find a bottle opener. The scissors didn't work and only resulted in me cutting my finger so Leicia rang down for room service and asked if they could find a bottle opener for us.

When the man brought the bottle opener up to the room, he noticed my finger was bleeding and asked if I wanted a plaster for it. It was only a small scratch but he went off and next thing there's a knock on the door and two dead fit, hunky looking young men standing there carrying an enormous first aid case. Leicia and Phoebe stared at them in amusement, wondering what all the fuss was about for a tiny little cut on my finger. Anyway, one of them put a plaster on my finger and the other one gave me some sterile wipes, just in case I needed them. Now, you would have to have been there because it was so funny especially the way they looked at Leicia and I. I had on tight fitting, black PVC trousers and Leicia was wearing a swirly black leather skirt. God knows what they thought of us or where we were going but all we could do was laugh! God, the men were so hunky in their black suits, mmm!

The taxi came for us shortly afterwards and took us to the Flux Museum in Chelsea. It's one of London's leading exhibition centres at the National Army Museum and curated by Linda Gray, the founder of Flux. From the moment we walked in, we were made to feel so welcome and fussed over. We were introduced to a lot of Mick's friends, old and new, but sadly we missed seeing Tom Hardy. We were offered wine or soft drinks and I, of course, chose wine! In fact, I had rather too much wine – as you can see in one of the photos of that day! I did get rather emotional at one point when I saw a painting of Mick which had been copied from a photo of him after he'd only been in prison for a short time. Again, it brought all the memories flooding back. We had such a lovely time there, seeing a lot of Mick's exhibited art work and chatting to lots of people until it was time to get in our taxi to take us back to the hotel. Leicia said everyone came out to wave us off, but I'm afraid I can't remember that bit owing to the wine making me forget, yes, it was the wine's fault!

When we got back to the hotel it was early evening and we decided to have a meal in our room. We called room service and I went and sat outside on the terrace taking in the view. As soon as our meals arrived, Leicia and Phoebe called me in and I stood up and walked right into the glass door. They said all you could hear was this loud bang when my head hit the door and then me staggering into the room with a glazed expression on my face. It practically knocked me out, even though Leicia and Phoebe and the waiter were concerned about me, they couldn't stop laughing. Well at least I kept them entertained even though I had a sore head. Again, it was the wine's fault!

After the meal, I decided I wanted to walk along the pathway beside the river. Leicia didn't want to go so Phoebe, bless her, said 'I'll go with you, Nan' much against Leicia's wishes. Phoebe said I was running along the path flapping my arms and shouting 'I'm a bird, I'm a bird'! For that night Phoebe said she was the adult and I was acting like a child. Oh well, never mind, I suppose I can't blame the wine for everything! Phoebe did get me back to our hotel room safely, where I immediately fell fast asleep.

The following morning we all awoke and got up early that Sunday morning as it was our last day and we wanted to fit in some more sight-seeing. We went down for our breakfast and Phoebe decided she wanted pancakes, but we were told they weren't served on a Sunday. However, the lovely waiter said as a special birthday treat for her, he would ask the chef to make some for her. Phoebe was thrilled and couldn't wait for them to arrive. When the waiter arrived back there were about six pancakes looking really pretty on the plate but, oh no, horrors, the chef had put summer berries on them! Well, Phoebe's face was a picture; the waiter was hovering waiting to see Phoebe's reaction. Leicia and I said 'Oh no, Phoebe, you're going to have to eat them after all the trouble they've gone to making them especially for you'. She picked up her knife and started to cut off the tiniest bit of pancake but her face was a picture of complete disgust even though it didn't have any berries on it, the mixture had the berries mixed in with it, which made it a big no-no for her. In the end, Leicia had to say to the waiter that Phoebe had not been well through the night and still had an upset stomach and was starting to feel unwell again. God, it was so embarrassing but we did laugh about it later – summer berries, bloody hell!

When we left the foyer to go sightseeing, there was a pop group being filmed with a gold Ferrari right outside. We watched the filming for a couple of minutes and then went on our way. We went past The Eye which didn't open til 11am, then we got on a tour bus. Phoebe insisted we went on the open top deck even though it was dead windy and absolutely freezing. We've never been so cold in our lives but quite a few sights were pointed out to us which made the cold bearable. We got off at Buckingham Palace, then made our way to Harrods and onto more designer shops that Phoebe wanted to visit. Phoebe then wanted to go to Costa for a coffee and a snack and I waited at our table whilst they went upstairs to the toilets. When they came back, I decided I wanted to go too. They gave me directions but, after finding the toilets (which were for men and women) I couldn't open the door to any of them. Back downstairs I went 'How do you open the toilet door' I asked them. They gave me more instructions and back I went upstairs. I twisted the door handle on one of the cubicles and pushed against the door. It was instantly pushed back again but not before I saw a gentleman sitting on the toilet with his trousers around his knees. He gave me a look to kill so I said to him 'You should have locked the door' and he said 'I did'. How I managed to open a locked door I don't know but when I went back to Leicia and Phoebe they thought it was hilarious. I still think the man hadn't locked the door properly.

After a freezing cold day of sightseeing in the capital, we went back to our hotel to collect our things and check out. Then we headed for Euston station to catch our train home. Euston was mad busy, there had been a parade in the city somewhere and as we got onto the escalators to go up, a woman and two girls with her, jumped on behind Phoebe which split our little group up so that Leicia and I were behind these people. The next thing we saw was Phoebe coming back down on an escalator. As she passed us in the opposite direction, I dropped my case and it went clattering down the escalator steps until it finally came to rest on this foreign gentleman's shoes, nestling perfectly on them. I looked down at him in horror. He never moved a muscle on his face or on his body, just stayed perfectly still. When he got to the top of the escalator he kicked my case off his feet, still without saying anything. Eehh, I thought, oh well, it was an accident.

We eventually arrived home safely all in one piece with a lot of funny memories to keep but if you ever meet Phoebe, never, ever mention Summer Berries to her. Ha Ha!

Chapter Nineteen: More Porridge Than Goldilocks

Mick always says he's ate more porridge than Goldilocks and the three bears and taken more hostages than Saddam Hussein but, despite this, he has always kept his sense of humour. He's also got a singing voice to die for and he is the six times winner of the Koestler Award for prison art. A very talented man indeed. In the past, he gained the reputation as the prison system's only serial hostage taker and during his very bad and mad phase when he was constantly tortured and kept locked inside an iron box concreted into the floor in the middle of his cell this was probably true. He used to say he had given more right hooks than he can remember and if you're going to have ago at him you'd better be prepared to knock him unconscious or kill him, as violence just makes him madder and stronger.

About 26 years ago, on one of the earlier times Mick had to go to court for sentencing, I wrote a letter to the judge presiding over the case to let him know that Mike and his family really needed him to be with them and to please be lenient with Mick and set him free. This strategy did work and the judge told Mick that because of my letter, he had decided to reduce the sentence he had intended to give him by two years – not a lot of time off really but it was a small step for Mick and he wrote me a lovely letter telling me about the judge's decision and thanking me for my part in it. Unfortunately, I can't find the letter but I'm sure it will turn up at some point. I've looked everywhere for it to no avail. I find this happening a lot to me lately, I'll just have to put it down to my age, I think!

Mick has another parole hearing coming up shortly, one which will be heard in public which is a great achievement for Mick or any other prisoner due for a parole hearing. Mick tells me there are lots of prisoners in prisons all around the country serving long sentences for rebelling against the system due to their harsh treatment whilst inside, just like him. I think it's disgusting that the prison system can do this to prisoners who have already served their time but are in fact doing what is in effect a life sentence. You see, most parole hearings are held inside prison and sometimes it's a foregone conclusion that there will be no parole if someone has rebelled against their treatment. Now the public can listen in to these hearings and there is much less chance of a no parole verdict. Everyone is keeping their fingers crossed for Mick. Oh God, I really, really hope he gets his parole, he so deserves to have a normal life on the outside after so many years locked up. A lot of people have written letters to Mick's solicitors to show support for him and I have also written a letter and Mick's solicitor has it in his possession ready for the hearing.

Many people only know about Mick's crimes through the media, reading reports that he has kicked off again. Mick's side of the story is, of course, never reported and the reason behind Mick's behaviour goes untold. It gives everyone the false impression that Mick is a very dangerous and disruptive man. A lot of people think Mick has spent so long inside because he's a mass murderer, or a terrorist and often say that to me. If he had committed any of those crimes he would have been released a long time ago

Mick now lives by a strong moral code and is very respected by a lot of the prison officers and prisoners alike. He is a completely changed man, for God's sake he's an old man now. He's a pensioner who forgets little things and has been known to put shaving foam on his toothbrush instead of toothpaste, bless him! He thinks he's my toy boy but doesn't realise he's so much older than me! It's our little joke, aah. He's not interested in crime anymore and don't forget, after he served his first prison sentence of seven years, the remaining years have just been added on and on because of his disruptive behaviour whilst in jail. This behaviour was undoubtedly aggravated by the inhumane way in which he has been treated in prison. There's an old saying that if you treat an animal with cruelty, it will eventually retaliate and bite you back.

As well as all Mick's charities, he set up an anti-knife campaign for young offenders. He set this up last year and called it 'Trash Knives not Lives' telling young criminals to pick up a paintbrush instead of a knife; why destroy lives when you can create something worthwhile. Only cowards carry knives, he says. He worked on this campaign with the help of friends on the outside. He also designed and had made a range of T shirts to raise awareness and to raise funds for the cause. The campaign produced a booklet which gives information and resources available in different areas. He is still hoping that his campaign will be used in secondary schools in the hope that it will make the would-be criminal stop and think about what he's about to embark on.

In the 60s before Mick went to jail, he and his friends used to have fights with other like-minded people just for the fun of it. No-one got seriously hurt and it would be forgotten about the next day. Sometimes the fights would be between mods and rockers. I remember all the mods on their scooters, they were fabulous with all those mirrors and fur on them. I was a mod, never a rocker, and Mick was a mod too. Most of the Neston lads were rockers though and they always picked fights with the mods from neighbouring Heswall but, as in Mick's fights, they never used knives or guns or were off their heads on drugs like they do these days. They used their fists and it was never about ganging up on one person; the numbers were always evened up and no-one was ever maimed or murdered. A few black eyes and broken noses, maybe, but that was about it, no-one died.

Mick's dad Joe used to teach boxing at a local gym and he always told Mick that whenever there was some trouble about to kick off, always get the first punch in and hope for the best. He's always lived by that code and it's got him through some really crazy times, he says. His best advice to all those kids on the street about to pick up a knife or a gun and running about in gangs is to watch the Krays film where the Kemp brothers play Reggie and Ronnie Kray. There's a bit at the end were they are old and grey after being locked up for years, standing handcuffed at their mother Violet's funeral because when you go inside, it's your family who suffers – your children, your parents, your wife, everyone who is left behind to carry on without you. They have to spend their lives travelling around the country to visit you. There's absolutely no glamour in crime; nothing at all but misery and unhappiness for everyone.

People are now beginning to find out the truth about Mick at long last. It's time for him to be released to live out what's left of his life without being caged. He just wants to feel freedom; the fresh air, the sun on his face, to see and smell flowers, to hear birdsong, to feel the sea and sand between his toes and to walk for miles with his two dogs which are to be called Reggie and Ronnie. He longs to do his artwork in a proper studio, on a proper canvas with proper paints in peace, perfect peace. It's time now for his release so that his lovely elderly mum Eira can know that her son is finally on the path to freedom before she passes away and I can give a huge sigh of relief that Mike can finally have his dad back in his life. Yes Mick, it's your time now to look out for Mike! Only joking Mike! FREE CHARLES BRONSON SALVADORE BORN AGAIN ARTIST! Hooray !!

It was Mick who suggested I write my story. He told me he had so much respect for me as a born survivor. Don't get me wrong though, I have often thought of writing my story. Many people have suggested it to me, a lot of people asking me over the years what Mick is really like but due to my anxiety and depression, the time never seemed right. I needed to be in a calm and peaceful frame of mind and as what is left of my divorce settlement from my 2nd husband fast running out and paying rent privately, I never seem to be in the right place until now to put my thoughts and recollections together. Anyway, I'm looking for a good, strong cardboard box to live in if my book doesn't sell! Mick always says to me 'Don't worry, Irene, I'll never let that happen to you'. There may be hope at the end of the tunnel for me

Chapter Twenty: The Future

Throughout the whole time Mick has been in prison, I have never once been nasty about him - yes, he made many, many mistakes in life but I have always supported him and had his back. Mike and I have also served his sentence. I've always hated the thought of him being cruelly beaten and tortured. When I was with Ian, he put on the Bronson film without my knowledge and I was so upset by all the violence and beatings Mick endured by the 'Heavy Mob' I had to ask Ian to turn it off. Ian for his part was upset that I was upset by Mick's treatment, he said ' oh, you're still in love with him, aren't you?'. Which is strange because when I appeared on the Trisha show, she also said she thought I was still in love with him, even though she knew I had remarried. Then, when I appeared on Loose Women with Paula, the night before Paula was asking me about Mick and she said to me the same thing 'You're still in loved with him, aren't you?' Well, am I or am I not? Maybe I'm still in love with the image of the man he used to be all those years ago. I do know that he still makes me laugh and cheers me up and helps me to stay positive. 'Always go to bed laughing, then, when you wake up you're smiling' he always says to me, and, yes, it does work.

Mick did say to me recently that you never forget you're first love, which I do think is true. He also told me that he had dreamt we remarried; he said the dream felt so real. He joked that if we did remarry, he would be my toyboy groom! Bless him, he still thinks he's younger than me! Funnily enough, I have also dreamt that we were going to remarry but in my dream I kept saying to him but your name is Salvadore, I don't know you, you're not Mick. Weird hey?! Mmmm? I wonder, will we or won't we, that's the question. I guess everyone will just have to wait to find out the answer to that one!

Every Friday Mick looks forward to a little treat. He is allowed a canteen on which he does a bit of shopping. In fact, he actually saved 85p last week by going for a cheaper brand. All good practice for when he comes out for good.

Chapter Twentyone: The End

Dear Readers (if there are any!),
Thank you for reading my story, it's only taken me about 15 years to write. I hope I have made you laugh and I hope I've made you sad and I hope I've given you an insight into life with a husband in jail and a celebrity criminal as well. There have been many times when I've not known if I was coming or going or if I'm already there but there is always light at the end of the tunnel, especially if you're prepared for the long wait.

Amidst all of the grief and upset, there are three good things which have come out of this Covid 19 pandemic:
1) It's given me the time to be able to write this book.
2) Mick has been given an open parole hearing after fighting many years for it
3) Best of all, Covid killed the Yorkshire Ripper, may he rest in Hell. God that sounds a bit cruel of me but it's only what he deserves anyway.

Take care, lots of love, Irene x
Oh no! Oh no! what now?! here we go again, nothing ever really changes. Oh well, I've been here many, many times in the past, I'll survive, I'm a survivor!

PS: Hi folks, I'm back again, just thought you would like to know a little secret of Mick's which he has never told anyone, even me, until the other week on the phone. He told me that every time he went out to do a robbery, he always wore a pair of my knickers to bring him luck and to make me feel close to him. Mmm, I wonder how many times they did bring him luck? Mick doesn't mind me sharing this secret with you. Bless him, but he is getting very forgetful at times, you know, due to his great age!

PPS: I've just remembered a little story that I would like to share with you. Sorry this is at the end and not the middle of my book. But this is totally me, I'm upside down and back to front but nevermind, hey!
One night, just before I got divorced from my second husband, Mike had popped in to see me. The next moment my ex arrived, he was shouting and swearing at me and Mike, so what did I do? I rang the police. I was afraid it was getting violent. I had my back to the front door and my ex was facing it when he stopped shouting and spoke in a quiet voice. As I lifted my arm one of the two policeman put a handcuff around my wrist, and yes, I was then taken to spend the night in a cell! What the hell! I was the one who had rang the police but my ex had seen the policemen enter the house and stopped shouting. Bloody hell, it was a nightmare. They didn't arrest me properly or take my fingerprints or anything else. They just put me in a cell! I was so upset, I cried all night, and I

remembered something that Mick used to do in his cell. He used to walk around and around counting the amount of times as he walked. This is something I did that night too. I was petrified. I have a fear of small rooms and lifts, etc and I really thought that I would be kept in prison forever, just like Mick because I was his ex. But thanks be to God they let me out the morning after and gave me a lift back home. Before I left the station one of the police officers said the reason I had been taken was because I lifted my arm up towards my ex and that can even count as assault. What a to do that was! After all, I had rung the police to deal with my ex. The following day a couple of my friends from Ethel Austin who had become police officers in the community were talking all about it. They couldn't believe what had happened to me as they knew me so well and knew about my ex's temper.
Just thought I'd share that little story with you!

This really is the end of my story. Look out for my next book, which Mick and I are doing together. It should be a good one.

Bye Irene xxx

PPPS: I made an onion cry!

Irene

Never give up on
Life.
Everyday is Magical.

At our Age we Are so
Lucky to Have our
Health.
The Dream goes on!

"Irene"

"
Never Did see it
the Soul Slipped Away,
Never Did Feel it,
Useless to Pray!
Never Did UNDErstAND
Guess I Never Will,
Never Did Taste the Tears
Reality is a Bitter Pill.
"

x

2021

SALVADOR 1314
C.S.C.
Woodhill·HMP

Bride Of Bronson DVD

Bronson and Me - Lee Wortley and Paula Salvador

BY LEE WORTLEY AND PAULA WILLIAMSON
FOREWORD BY CHARLES SALVADOR

In 2017 Paula Williamson, an actress and voice-over artist from Stoke stepped through the prison gates of 'Monster Mansion' in Wakefield and said "I do" to one of the world's most legendary and animated inmates.
Unfortunately their union was short lived after all hell broke loose over a misunderstanding that occurred during a trip to Tenerife.
This book is a tell-all expose of the collateral damage that ensued in its wake. A chronological trip through the events of their marriage, a metaphorical box-ticker of dos and don'ts for anyone treading a similar path.
Lee Wortley worked with Paula on her book, right up to the time of her premature passing, before taking up the task of its painstaking completion.
This story will shock, surprise and infuriate you.

Available now from www.badboysbooks.net